IMAGES
of America

NEWNAN

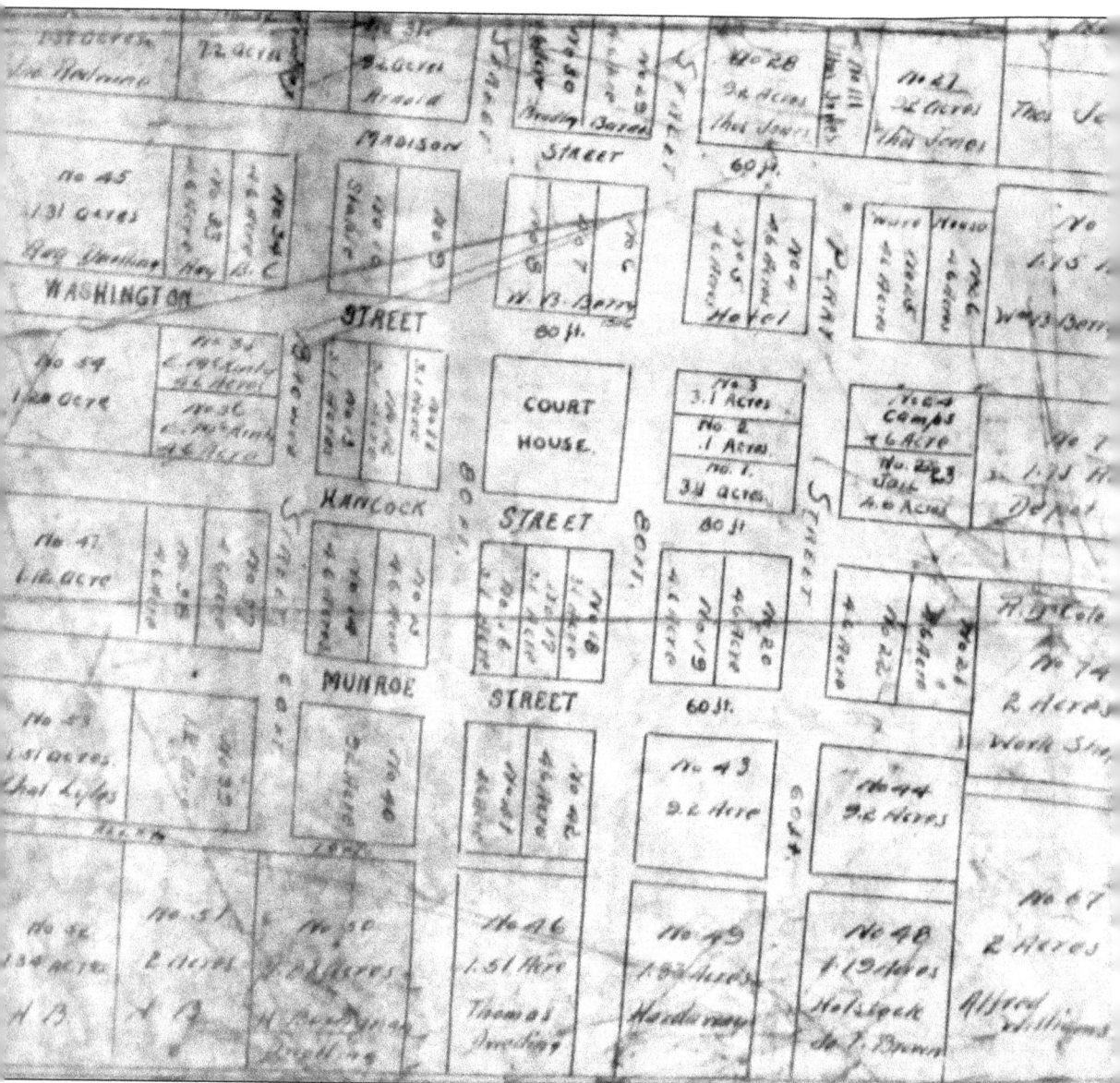

This is a 1923 copy of a 19th-century map of downtown Newnan, showing the locations of the historic courthouse, businesses and hotels around the Court Square, the Male Academy lot, the homes of Congressman Hugh Buchanan and other local residents, and other sites from the period. (Courtesy of the Newnan-Coweta Historical Society.)

ON THE COVER: Employees of the R.D. Cole Manufacturing Company, named for Robert Dukes Cole, gather at a home on East Broad Street. A souvenir booklet printed by the company in 1904 to commemorate its 50th anniversary states that R.D. Cole moved to Newnan in 1849 to practice the cabinetmaking trade. In 1854, he formed the firm of Cole & Barnes with Thomas Barnes, and the company eventually evolved into R.D. Cole & Co. By 1904, the company employed 535 people and its boiler plant was called "the largest and most complete in the South." Most homes in and around downtown Newnan were built with materials from the Cole plant. (Courtesy of the Newnan-Coweta Historical Society.)

IMAGES
of America

NEWNAN

W. Jeff Bishop

ARCADIA
PUBLISHING

Published by Arcadia Publishing
Charleston, South Carolina

Library of Congress Control Number: 2014937544

For all general information, please contact Arcadia Publishing:
Telephone 843-853-2070
Fax 843-853-0044
E-mail sales@arcadiapublishing.com
For customer service and orders:
Toll-Free 1-888-313-2665

Visit us on the Internet at www.arcadiapublishing.com

Dedicated to my wife, Barbara

CONTENTS

ACKNOWLEDGMENTS

The Newnan-Coweta Historical Society began in 1971 at the home of Dr. and Mrs. John Wells, where "several concerned citizens discussed the urgent need of preserving and protecting historical homes and buildings of the community," according to one local history. The late Herb Bridges was its first president, and I thank him for collecting, identifying, and preserving so many images of Newnan and Coweta County's past, some of which are included in this volume. Through the decades, many board members, volunteers, and employees of the Newnan-Coweta Historical Society have put in countless hours of work to tell Newnan's story and preserve its rich history. I specifically thank Dorothy Pope, Elizabeth Beers, JoAnn Ray, Georgia Shapiro, Keri Adams, Pamela Prange, Sarah LaMance, Tom Camp, Laurie Pope, Tom Redwine, Carlisle Young, and Joanna Arietta, without whom this volume would not have been possible.

I thank the *Newnan Times-Herald* newspaper, its owners, and its staff for their role in recording the town's past and for their commitment to its continued preservation.

I thank my acquisitions editor at Arcadia Publishing, Liz Gurley, for guiding me through this long process and giving me assistance when I needed it.

I thank Dr. Sarah Hill, archaeologist Jim Langford, and my grandmother Jackie Robinson Jones for infecting me with the "history bug," from which I may never recover. I thank Drs. Ann McCleary and Keith Hebert of the University of West Georgia Center for Public History for their guidance.

Most of all, I wish to thank my wife and children, who support me in everything I do, even when the hours are long and the task is onerous. I love you all so very much.

Unless otherwise noted, all images are courtesy of the Newnan-Coweta Historical Society.

INTRODUCTION

"We had no schools nor churches, and we were all living on dirt floors or split puncheons to our cabins, with one door and one room for cooking, eating and sleeping, and nearly all of us barefooted in summer from necessity of money to buy shoes." This is the primitive Newnan remembered by its first historian and pioneer citizen, William U. Anderson, a former postmaster, hotelkeeper, and blacksmith who meticulously chronicled the names of all the young town's newspapers, businesses, schools, and other institutions. If a street moved or had a change in name, Anderson took note of it, and when a wooden building burned and was replaced with something modern and brick, or even just changed owners, Anderson would add it to his growing encyclopedia of Newnan trivia. Anderson compiled lists of the town's legislators, judges, lawyers, merchants, doctors, prominent citizens, and even the not-so-prominent ones he thought worthy of mention in his brief 1880 survey of the tiny West Georgia town.

"We then rocked our children in hollow-log cradles; men, women and children would walk five miles barefooted to a Saturday night frolic, dance all night and go home with the gals in the morning. We then thought we were as big as big Indian and as proud as anyone now with their red calico dress with a dozen tucks. All then nearly wore our own homespun. We felt proud of it, too; for it was home manufactory . . . But we soon began to improve."

Before steam power became prevalent, "everything was hand work." Anderson writes, "We made our wagons, carts, and all our plows, axes, farming tools at home. We had our smoke-houses at home, and corn-cribs in our horse lots, and if a neighbor had to buy corn or meat . . . he went to his neighbor and got his supplies."

It is a different Newnan now. According to the US Census Bureau, Coweta County added 38,102 new residents between 2000 and 2010, bringing its total population to 127,317. Newnan doubled its population over the most recent decade, to 33,039. "That was a surprise to us," Newnan mayor Keith Brady told the *Times-Herald* newspaper when it reported the new figures. "We knew we had grown, but we did not think it was going to be a double number."

What makes Newnan attractive to newcomers is an "obvious answer," he said. While many downtown areas have languished, Newnan has retained the integrity of its historical core, even as longtime downtown shopping venues transformed into eateries and old movie theaters became pizza places and churches. "What we offer here, as a city, not only provides opportunities for shopping, eating and recreation for our citizens, but it does things like attract newcomers, and business, like the Cancer Treatment Centers of America. The most important thing we focus on as a council is to build quality of life that makes generations want to come back here."

Change is inevitable, but Newnan has never lost sight of its origins, and its people have worked diligently to preserve its history, especially its architectural history, according to Georgia Shapiro, a local preservationist who was instrumental in identifying many local historical buildings. These structures add to the "character of the community," Shapiro said. "You ride through all these little towns, and so many of them have lost their soul. You don't understand the community because their neighborhoods are gone." Shapiro remembers a group from a movie production company that drove from Charleston to Newnan and told her they were "dumbfounded that Newnan is so unique" in having so many old homes. "'We thought every Southern town looked like Newnan,' they told me."

There is a reason why Newnan is known as the "City of Homes," Shapiro said. "And it did not happen by itself. A lot of people have worked really hard to make it this way. And I am so proud of what we have accomplished."

This is the pictorial story, then, of Newnan's gradual evolution from backwater frontier town to a thriving metropolitan hub, and today's historical "City of Homes."

One

McIntosh to Bullsboro

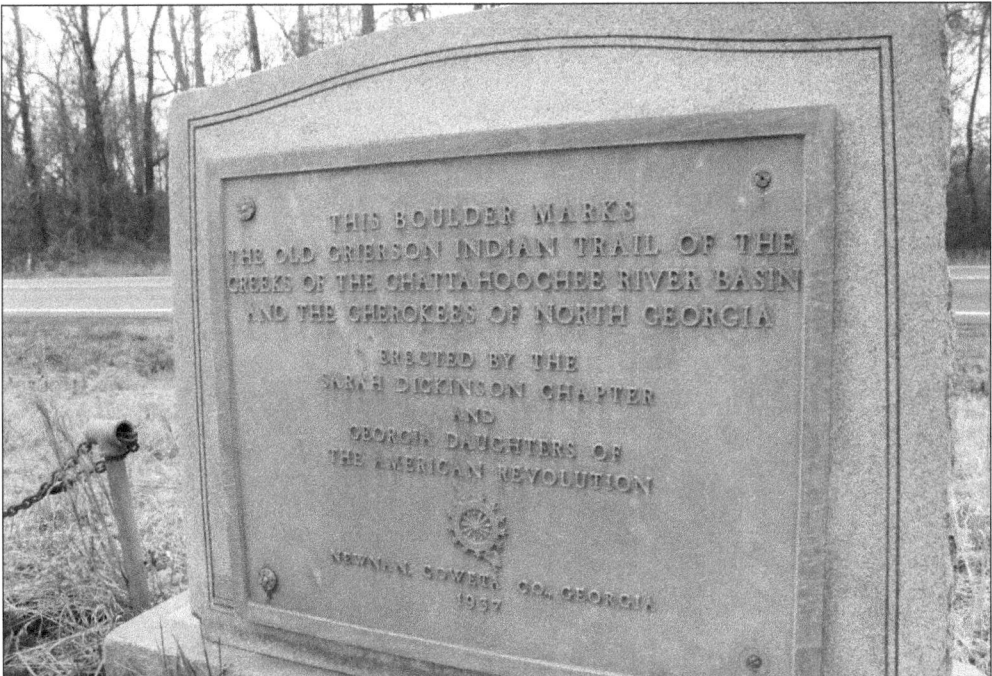

Early historian William U. Anderson described Newnan as a "wilderness," but, in fact, it was strategically located in February 1828 at a productive spring near the convergence of several major trading routes, most notably the McIntosh Road and the Grierson Trail. These routes, congruent with ancient trails, had been widened into wagon roads and used by Native Americans and whites alike for years prior to Newnan's settlement.

The Chattahoochee River, bordering the new county of Coweta, along with the river's many tributaries, had been home to the Creek Indians and their ancestors, Muskogee-speaking peoples, for many thousands of years. Towns were typically located along major waterways, with large earthen mounds serving as ceremonial and civic centers. The Piedmont and its resources had been carefully managed by these early occupants.

High school textbooks for generations have perpetuated the myth of intrepid white pioneers taming a vast, uncharted, and untamed wilderness, but the last truly virgin landscape in North America would have existed during the Pleistocene epoch, which ended about 11,700 years ago, soon after bands of hunter-gatherers crossed into the Americas from Siberia. Almost as soon as they came here, these Paleo-Indians were also transforming the environment by hunting megafauna, creating trails, crafting tools, and gathering mast, as illustrated in this 16th-century engraving by Theodor de Bry.

These prehistoric people left behind many artifacts that are still commonly found in local fields, including practical tools like spear points, arrowheads, and grinding stones. Later cultures such as the Woodland and Mississippian crafted complex works of art from wood, stone, tortoiseshell, quartz, and copper that were often included in burials of high-status people.

The McIntosh Trail was at one time the backbone of a constantly evolving trade and transportation network stretching from the Ocmulgee River to the Alabama state line and beyond. The trail's namesake was William McIntosh, an entrepreneur and Lower Creek leader who was denounced as a traitor and executed for unlawfully ceding Creek lands for his own personal profit in 1825. The McIntosh Trail connected McIntosh's holdings on the Chattahoochee River with his various other places of business, including the Indian Springs Hotel in Butts County.

The people living on the eastern bank of the Chattahoochee River, in what is now Coweta County, awoke to a horrifying sight on the morning of April 30, 1825. What is now McIntosh Reserve Park, on the Carroll County side of the Chattahoochee River, was in flames that morning. Alexander Ware describes the chaos in a hastily written letter from his home on Line Creek: "Several neighbors of mine, who lodged on the bank of the Chattahoochie, this side of McIntosh's, about daybreak heard the war-whoop, and they suppose from two to four hundred guns were fired; the houses were on fire when they set off." This portrait of McIntosh is featured at the Newnan Historic Depot.

"At daylight, on Saturday morning last, hundreds of the hostiles surrounded our house, and instantly murdered General McIntosh and Tome Tustunnuggee, by shooting near one hundred balls into them," wives Peggy and Susannah McIntosh write in a letter. Chilley McIntosh and Moody Kennard escaped by jumping out of a window. The attackers "then Commenced burning and plundering in the most unprincipalled way," the widows write, "so that here I am driven from the Ashes of my smoking dwelling, left with nothing but my poor Naked hungry Children."

Francis Flournoy, a white witness to the executions of McIntosh and his allies, said in a sworn statement on May 16, 1825, that "as soon as they had closely surrounded the general's dwelling-house, and fixed a guard round the house which I was in, set fire to the dwelling-house, and immediately shot the general, who instantly fell, and was drawn out of the house, with considerable effect of the flames; and they continued firing at his corpse, until, I think, they had shot more than fifty balls into him." Wife Peggy McIntosh wrote soon afterward, "I do not blame the Creeks . . . It was by Government my husband lost his life. Government say to my husband . . . 'Go to Arkansas and you will be better off.' My husband wished to please the Government. My home is burned. Myself and children run. My children naked, no bread, on blanket is all. Like some stray dog I suffer. With one blanket I cover my three children and myself. The government say 'Go!' The Indians kill him. Between two fires my husband dies."

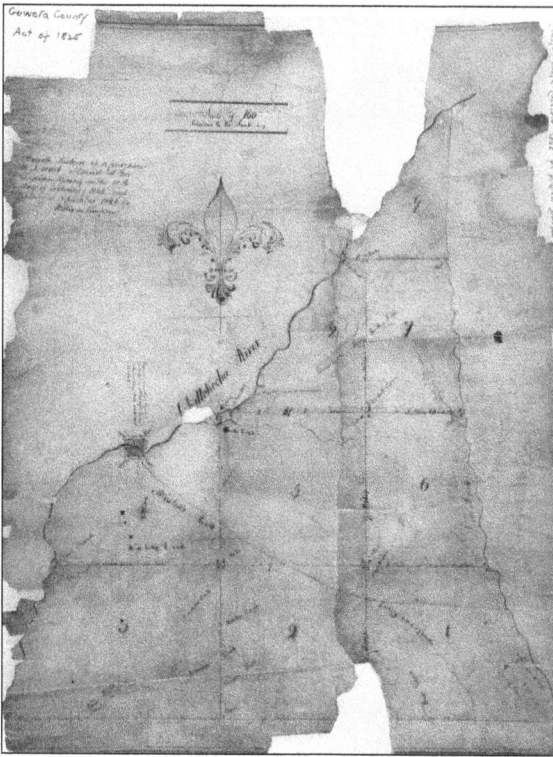

Coweta County
Act of 1825

In 1825, Coweta County was formed, named for the Lower Creek tribe McIntosh helped lead. Coweta originally had nine districts and "extended up to near Sandtown, then in the county of DeKalb" (it is now in Fulton County), early historian and settler W.U. Anderson records. The land was surveyed in 1826. "We don't know of but one man now living on the same land he settled on in the fall of 1826, and he lived there ever since," Anderson writes in 1880. Christopher B. Brown was at that time "well and healthy in his eightieth year," he writes. "All others there were here . . . are either dead or moved away."

Bullsborough, the first county seat of Coweta, was established in 1826–1827, "two and one-half miles north-east of Newnan, on the Fayetteville road, at which place the first election was held," according to W.U. Anderson. The Daughters of the American Revolution erected this marker in 1925 in recognition of the centennial of the organization of the county. Pictured is Mary Gibson Jones, coauthor of *Coweta County Chronicles*, an early history of the county. "The pioneers lived in tents at first, and in one roomed log cabins," Jones reports in *Chronicles*. "The first jail in the county is said to have been a hollow poplar tree, but whether it was at Bullsboro or Newnan" no one recorded.

Two

NEWNAN BEGINS

W.U. Anderson writes that he "purchased a lot in Newnan" at the initial sale in 1828 and "moved to Newnan one month afterwards for permanent settlement." At the time of the initial sale, that particular stretch of the McIntosh Trail was occupied by "two squatter settlers," William A. Hicks and James Caldwell, who "both had houses of entertainment for travelers." All that existed of the Newnan Square was "a log cabin . . . with a store," Anderson records. "The number of travelers over the roads and Indian trails was very great—so great that one person related that her father removed from his home on the main road and established another where he would not be called upon so frequently to entertain travelers," write Mary Gibson Jones and Lily Reynolds in *Coweta County Chronicles*.

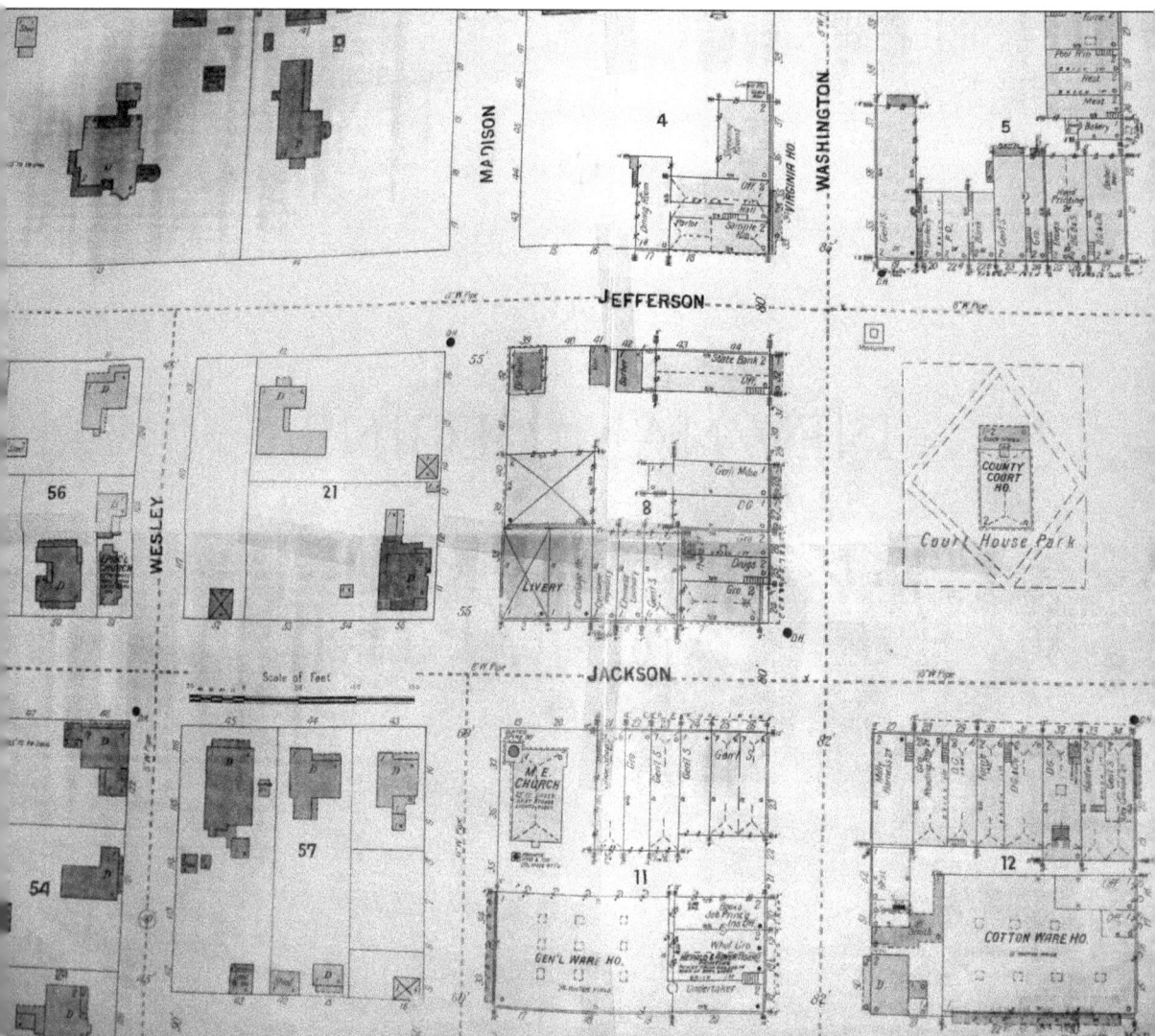

Named for Gen. Daniel Newnan of North Carolina, the new city of Newnan was established with Thomas Roney as its first postmaster. The new town included carpenters, storekeepers, blacksmiths, lawyers, doctors, merchants, hotelkeepers, brickmasons, and sawmill operators. Presbyterian and Methodist churches were organized. Lots were sold beginning on March 25, 1828, with prices ranging from $40 up to $611.50. A Dr. J. Palmore taught the first school in town, established at the log courthouse on the square, but he was soon succeeded by attorney Thomas A. Latham. The first recorded death in Newnan occurred that year, when Leonard Griffin, a traveling carpenter, came through town and became ill.

The Dr. A.B. Calhoun home on Greenville Street was built in the 1850s and constructed of handmade brick. For many years, the home was considered the "showplace of Newnan." The home was demolished in 1955 to make way for a shopping center. The site is now the home of the Coweta County Justice Center.

The original log courthouse on the Newnan square was replaced by a brick courthouse in 1829. The courthouse, which originally did not include the clock tower shown here, was built by William Hitchcock, who constructed similar structures all over the state. The building, a combination of brick vernacular and Greek Revival architecture, stood on the square for 75 years. The brickmason, John D. Brown, and his principal carpenter, Mercer Babb, became Newnan citizens after the project was completed. This photograph was taken in 1885.

College Temple, built in 1853, was located between College and Kellogg Streets and Temple Avenue. The college for women, chartered in 1854, was the first female college to offer a master of arts degree. "This will long be remembered by many, who . . . graduated and taught in it," recalls Anderson. Its founder, Moses P. Kellogg, came to Newnan "almost penniless," says Anderson, but he managed to attract about 100 students per year to the school, many of whom were "taught without fee or reward, except to feel and know that none have been turned down for their poverty." College Temple, which closed in 1888, "added more to Newnan than any other institution in the place," Anderson says, and was "the result of an individual, by his own exertions, and from the patronage given him by his merits as a teacher."

Buena Vista, built originally in the 1830s by John Thomas as a small cottage, is one of Newnan's oldest and grandest homes. Edward Storey later purchased the house and expanded it significantly. The Greek Revival style was typical of mid-19th-century upper-class homes in Newnan. All early portions of the residence have heart pine floors and ceilings. Rep. Hugh Buchanan lived in the home for many years.

The Arnold-Arnall Home, at 34 College Street, is Newnan's oldest home still located at its original site. George Scott originally built the house in 1830, and tracts from the lot later formed the College-Temple Historic District. James Arnold doubled the size of the residence in 1872. It was the home of Henry and Sallie Arnall, grandparents of Georgia governor Ellis Arnall, for 50 years. Henry was president of Wahoo Manufacturing Company and the director of Newnan National Bank. The home features a Greek Revival influence through its four-columned front porch and cantilevered balcony.

The Joseph Ephraim and Elizabeth Steagall Dent Home, located at 52 College Street, was saved from the bulldozers in the 1950s, when plans called for it to be the location of a new high school. The home is one of only about 22 antebellum houses remaining in Newnan. The Greek Revival–style home has four large, fluted Doric columns and a cantilevered balcony.

Residence P. L. Sutherland, Newnan, Ga.   401,60

Built in the mid-19th century in what was then considered "out in the country," this home on Bullsboro Drive, formerly Jefferson Street, now serves as Hillcrest Chapel Funeral Home. Businessman John B. Wilcoxon had the home constructed in 1852 and lived here until 1896. Wilcoxon, with H.J. Sargent, built the first cotton manufacturing plant in Sargent, which made cotton rope. In 1888, the company was purchased and renamed Wahoo Manufacturing Company. Hillcrest Chapel acquired and converted the residence in 1953. The house was originally part of the Shadowlawn plantation.

This home, once located at the corner of West Washington and College Streets, was built by the same family that gave its name to Ray Park. Judge John Ray had the house built soon after his arrival in 1828. It was his residence until 1868, when it was sold to Dr. J.H. Hall, a Baptist pastor. Nurse Fannie A. Beers called the Ray home "a complete rendezvous for convalescing soldiers" during the Civil War. The photograph above was likely taken in 1885, while the photograph below was taken in 1876.

Three

THE CIVIL WAR

Because of its location on the West Point Railroad and its distance from the front lines of battle, Newnan was selected as a hospital location during the Civil War. The hospital eventually took over the entire downtown district, including all of the large buildings on the Court Square, even the Coweta County Courthouse lawn, on which 100-foot-long sheds were constructed. The local church buildings were also used; only the Newnan First Methodist Church was left open for services. The courthouse was penetrated by the Federal guns of the 18th Indiana Artillery on July 30, 1864. (Courtesy of Martin Pate.)

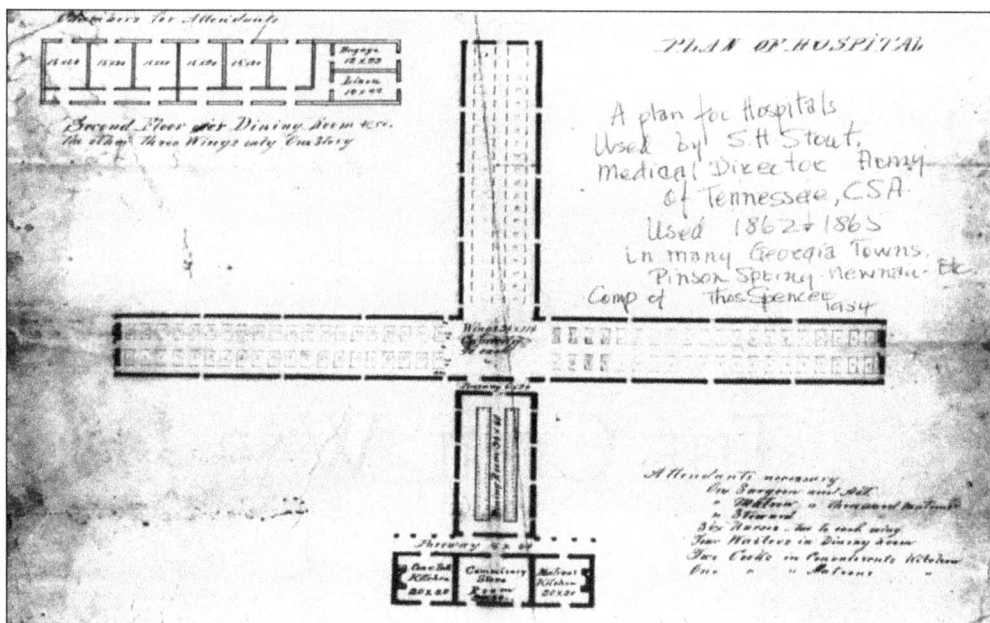

Over 10,000 Confederate sick and wounded were brought to Newnan to be treated at the seven local hospitals—Bragg, Buckner, College Temple, Coweta House, Foard, Gamble, and Pinson Springs. These men fought at various battles in Tennessee, the Battle of Chickamauga, and in the engagements that formed the Atlanta Campaign. A total of 269 of these men are buried at Oak Hill Cemetery in the Confederate section.

Fannie A. Beers, a nurse for the Confederacy, wrote while she was stationed in Newnan that "the whole town was converted into hospitals, and every eligible place filled with sick." Local residents "strove in every way to add to their comfort." Every train that came into town was "freighted with human misery," Beers writes. "In the Buckner Hospital alone there were nearly a thousand beds, tenanted by every conceivable form of suffering." The patients' "piteous moans filled the air," Beers says. (Courtesy of Martin Pate.)

Coweta delegates to the Georgia Secession Convention were (clockwise from top left) Dr. A.B. Calhoun, Maj. William B. Shell, and Joseph J. Pinson. The vote was taken on January 19, 1861, with all Coweta delegates voting in favor of seceding from the Union. "The action of the convention . . . is well remembered by most every child in the country," writes Anderson in his history.

Written on the back of this photograph is "Jos. W. Parks, Killed July 1st 1862. Malvern Hill." Pvt. Joseph W. Parks enlisted on July 30, 1861, in the Coweta Guards, a part of the 7th Georgia Infantry. This letter from home on May 10, 1861, discourages Parks from joining the service and instructs him to remain in school at Emory College: "[We] think it is the least you can do apply yourself and improve the opportunity afforded and not be talking about wanting to go home like a little 10 year old boy and suffering your mind to be diverted because there is an excitement in the country." According to his military records, Parks was wounded at Malvern Hill, Virginia, on July 1, 1862, but he did not die from those wounds until reaching Richmond, Virginia, 10 days later, on July 11, 1862. He was 18 years old.

Seen here is "Josiah G.W. Latimer, 'Co. A' 7th Ga. Regt. Infantry, Killed 2nd Manassas, Aug. 31st, 1862." According to W.U. Anderson, Coweta "furnished the first company in the regiment from the state of Georgia." The Coweta Guards served alongside the Paulding Volunteers, the DeKalb Light Infantry, the Iverson Invincibles, the Cobb Mountaineers, and the Franklin Volunteers.

Seen at right and below, Confederate colonel George H. Carmical, a Newberry, South Carolina, native, moved to Newnan in 1852 and enlisted with the Coweta Guards, 7th Georgia Infantry, at the age of 19 in May 1861. "With nine others the company was mustered into service . . . and sent forward at once to Harpers Ferry, Va.," Carmical writes in *Coweta County Chronicles*. He moved up to second lieutenant on May 31 and to captain on December 16. Carmical says he "participated in nearly every battle fought by the Army of Northern Virginia." Carmical was promoted to major at the Battle of Malvern Hill, on July 1, 1862. He remained with the regiment through the Battle of Gettysburg, and he was wounded in battle at Knoxville on December 4, 1863. "In four years being seriously wounded twice and slightly wounded once," he recalls. Carmical was elected colonel on July 27, 1864.

Cincinnatus C. Wilson enlisted as a private in the Coweta Guards, Company A, 7th Regiment, on July 30, 1861. He made it to the rank of corporal before he was killed at Knoxville on December 4, 1863.

Also killed at Knoxville from the Coweta Guards, Company A, 7th Regiment, was Lt. Jacob N. Bedenbaugh. After enlisting as a private on May 31, 1861, Bedenbaugh was appointed second sergeant on July 16, 1862. He was elected junior second lieutenant on July 20, 1862, and second lieutenant in April 1863. He was killed at Knoxville on November 28, 1863.

Thomas J. Pinson was "a promising young lawyer," writes W.U. Anderson in his history. Killed in battle in 1862 while serving in the Coweta Guards, Pinson was "well remembered by his friends and community." He is buried at Oak Hill Cemetery.

Capt. Ansley Moses served in Company D, 53rd Regiment. He was born on April 9, 1829, two miles from Senoia. "Ansley Moses, a farmer and teacher, built in 1857 a home on a large plantation . . . half way between Turin and Sharpsburg," Mary Gibson Jones and Lily Reynolds report in *Coweta County Chronicles*. "He was opposed to secession, but when Georgia seceded he enlisted at once, helped organize Co. D, 53rd Ga. Regt., of which he was made captain and was with Lee in Virginia campaigns until wounded at Gettysburg."

The Passolt House, at 148 Greenville Street, housed Confederate officers during the Civil War. The home, built in the early 1860s, has been moved back from the road and significantly remodeled since this photograph was taken in 1909. The original roadbed of the McIntosh Trail runs beside the house. Resident Albert A. Passolt was hired by the City of Newnan to design and build a modern waterworks and electric system for the city. Pictured are the Passolt children, Catherine Passolt Glass and Margaret Passolt Moody, with their nanny, whose name is not known.

Confederate Medal of Honor recipient William Thomas Overby grew up east of Newnan, in a home where Highway 34 is now located. Markers commemorate Overby at the homesite and at the county courthouse. Overby served with Mosby's Rangers during the Civil War and was hanged following his capture at Front Royal, Virginia, when he refused to reveal the hiding place of Mosby's men.

John Addison Story, born about 1838 on Story Hill, near Mount Carmel Methodist Church, enlisted as a private in Company K, 1st Georgia Cavalry Regiment, in the Army of Tennessee. He returned to his wife, Susan Elizabeth Kidd, following the war, and they had nine children. Story died in 1910.

Newnan was remote from the battlefront until Saturday morning, July 30, 1864, when Gen. Edward M. McCook approached Newnan from the east. Nurse Kate Cumming writes in her journal that the locomotive at the station "gave a most un-earthly whistle, and immediately we heard the firing of musketry . . . I never saw men run as all did . . . two or three shots whizzed past me . . . I went to look at the fighting. I had just got out when we heard shouting that 'the Yankees were running!'" (Courtesy of Martin Pate.)

As McCook withdrew his forces and headed southwest of Newnan, Confederate general Joseph Wheeler entered Newnan and set up his headquarters at Buena Vista, at 87 LaGrange Street. Pickets were established to guard the city as Wheeler, and his cavalry went south of town to engage McCook at what would become known as the Battle of Brown's Mill. The battle provided a rare victory for the South in the Atlanta Campaign. "The dead lay all around us on every side, single and in groups and piles," writes Confederate nurse Fannie Beers. "Some lay as if peacefully sleeping; others, with open eyes seemed to glare at anyone who bent above them. Two men lay as they had died, the 'Blue' and the 'Gray' clasped in a fierce embrace. What had passed between them could never be known." (Both, courtesy of Martin Pate.)

This photograph, taken on July 4, 1920, shows three Civil War veterans from Coweta County—from left to right, Ira Brantley "Dock" Banks, Leander Rollins Banks, and William Hubbard Banks. Their father, Levi Banks, joined the state militia at age 59, along with his five sons, two of whom died during the war. These three brothers were at Appomattox Courthouse when Gen. Robert E. Lee surrendered. The brothers recalled that Lee was standing under an apple tree when he surrendered, and "every limb and twig" of the tree was "cut to pieces" as the men took home bits of it as souvenirs. "Even the ground had been dug up all around and every root was taken." The middle brother, Leander, wore a beard after the Civil War to hide the scars from when he was shot in the face. During the surrender, he was being hauled in an ambulance of the 53rd Georgia. The brothers recalled stacking their guns and then walking all the way back home to Senoia.

The photograph at left shows W.O. Perry as he went off to war in 1862, at age 17. The photograph below shows Perry at age 63, in 1908. "Our soldiers all returned home and began to take on citizenship again after a four years war, many of them without a dollar to begin with," writes W.U. Anderson in his history. "But to their credit they did not set down to grieve over their losses and the lost cause, but . . . some of them made good crops, and our county has steadily improved ever since, and in a few years more we will be all right and the losses of the war will be passed over as a thing forgotten, and our country will be prosperous and happy if we will only persevere."

Four

INDUSTRY AND EDUCATION

After the Civil War, a statue was erected at the intersection of Washington and Jefferson Streets to honor the Confederate dead. The monument, 22 feet high and weighing 16 tons, was later relocated to the front of the new Coweta County Courthouse, constructed in June 1904. This photograph, taken about 1903, shows the statue facing south, with the East Court Square to the left.

The "Goober" passenger train was a familiar sight on the Atlanta & West Point Railroad in Newnan in the late 19th and early 20th centuries. The first railroad cars came to town in 1852. Among the first six directors of the railroad were Newnan residents Joel Wingfield Terrell and Andrew Berry.

The Male Academy was constructed in 1883 by Charles Leavell Moses, son of Ansley Moses. The school was fabricated from a church building that had been relocated from the corner of College and Wesley Streets. The building was later moved when the Newnan public schools began operation. It was rediscovered and restored in the 1970s and currently serves as a museum for the city. The Newnan-Coweta Historical Society operates the Male Academy Museum today.

Constructed in the 1860s on the northeast corner of the Court Square, the brick building known as the Virginia House served for a century as Newnan's downtown hotel. Originally called the Coweta Hotel or the McDowell House, it was erected by a tinsmith named William Reynolds after the previous building at the location had burned to the ground. He sold the building soon after it was completed and moved west. The structure was purchased by Eleanor Cunningham Yancey and Rowena Ann Yancey, newly arrived from Boydtown, Virginia, in 1865 to visit their sister. The sisters named the 14-room hotel after their home state.

This photograph shows East Broad Street in 1885. Note the old depot on the right, with the 19th-century courthouse clock tower in the background. On the left is the R.D. Cole Company building. The company began in 1850 "on a one-horse scale," according to W.U. Anderson's history. It acquired a small engine in 1852 and expanded its business, operating for more than a century at the same location on East Broad Street (Depot Street). Many, if not most, of the homes in Newnan are built with materials manufactured by the R.D. Cole Company.

The Olympia Hotel was located until about 1910 at the current site of the post office on Greenville Street. It was one of a number of hotels in downtown Newnan, including the Virginia House, which remained a hotel well into the 20th century.

This view of the North Court Square in the 1890s shows a time when cotton was still king in Coweta County. A postcard bearing this image is inscribed, "Dear Mother, this is some cotton country, all you can see is cotton."

This is a scene from *Coweta County Chronicles*. No information is given about the location of this cotton field, but it shows that work opportunities for many African Americans were often limited to the same types of physical labor they had been forced to undertake during slavery.

Dr. John Henry Jordan (1870–1912) was a trailblazer, becoming the first African American doctor in the city of Newnan. He operated his practice from an office on Pinson Street.

The John Jordan home, constructed in 1908, is located at 61 Pinson Street. The house is part of the Chalk Level neighborhood, a traditionally African American community southeast of the Court Square. Chalk Level has been described as the "nexus of African-American life" in the 19th and early 20th centuries.

This photograph shows Dr. John Henry Jordan and his family in 1911. In addition to operating his medical practice, Dr. Jordan organized a medical aid organization devoted to teaching health and hygiene. He was part owner of a general store and the owner of a sawmill, and also invested in real estate and rented property to local families. Pictured, from left to right, are (first row) Mollie R. Jordan, Dr. Jordan, and their son Edward P. Jordan; (second row) Gertrude Ramsey Randolph, Joseph Randolph, and an unidentified family friend.

Newnan attorney William Yates Atkinson was governor of Georgia for two 2-year terms from 1894 to 1898. He was a supporter of education, authoring legislation to establish what is now Georgia College and State University in Milledgeville. He was also a reformer, hiring the first female salaried employee at the state capitol and becoming an outspoken opponent of the practice of lynching. He pardoned Adolphus Duncan, an African American man wrongly convicted of raping a white woman, and he was one of the few men who tried to stop the lynching of Sam Hose in Newnan, one of the most notorious lynchings in American history. Atkinson is pictured here with his wife, Susan Cobb Milton Atkinson.

The Newnan Presbyterian Church was built for $8,000 on a lot donated by Harrison J. Sargent. The church was dedicated on February 13, 1873. The Newnan Presbyterian Church was first organized with 15 charter members on June 21, 1828, at Bullsboro. For six years, services were held in a log building; in 1834, it relocated to what is now 67 Jackson Street. In 1854, a new building was erected on the lot now occupied by McKoon Funeral Home, at 38 Jackson Street. It moved to the present site, on Salbide Avenue and Greenville Street, in 1872.

The Newnan First United Methodist Church was constructed in 1927. Work crews can be seen on top of the steeple. The first church building was near what is now Oak Hill Cemetery, on Jefferson Street. A wooden church was later built at 31 Wesley Street in about 1830. The building, 30 feet square, was located on two acres. It was enlarged and given a steeple in 1855. A brick building was then constructed on the southwest corner of Jackson and Madison Streets, and the old wooden building was repurposed as the Male Academy (now the Male Academy Museum). The current building was completed in 1928.

This photograph of Central Baptist Church in Newnan was taken around the turn of the 20th century. On July 25, 1897, a group of 144 people met at the old opera house on the South Court Square to form a church "to keep house for God and to expand God's kingdom," according to the *History of Coweta County, Georgia*. The first pastor was Dr. J.H. Hall. The lot, at the corner of West Broad and Brown Streets, was obtained in September 1897.

This photograph shows the Newnan High School junior class in 1924–1925. J.V. Waites was the principal, and B.F. Pickett was the superintendent of schools. By 1903, the graduating class at Newnan High had grown to 79 students.

The Newnan High School ninth-grade class is shown in here around 1925. Newnan residents continued to vote for bond issues for new schools, and the county continued to finance education in the face of the repeated failure of the state to produce the funds necessary to support the schools.

The Newnan High School class of 1909, seen here in June, includes, from left to right, (first row) Kimball Mooney, Lucile Lovelady, Florrie Virginia Stephens, and Willie Bohannon; (second row) Mary Hazel Sago, Lorn Hall McKoy, Stella Pauline Wadsworth, May Cole, and Albert Sidney Camp; (third row) Mary Louise Reaves, Ruth Mae Owens, Robert Hill Freeman, John James Farmer, Mary Elizabeth Daniel, Tom Pope Goodwyn, and Fannie Hill Herring.

McClelland Academy was a private school for African American students located on Duncan Street, across from the current city swimming pool site. This photograph of the class of 1929 includes, from left to right, (seated) the Rev. Franklin Gregg (principal), Katie Lee Neely, Willena Thompkins, Thelma Williams (Harris), and Pearl Stargell; (standing) Joe Woods, Leila Hines, Tommy Dallas, Jennie Shirley, John Dodds, Sallie Kate Terrell, and Lola Smith (Evans).

This photograph of the 1926 graduating class of McClelland Academy includes, from left to right, (seated) Mildred Wilson, Louise McColumn, Sallie P. Leigh, and Maude Maxey; (standing) Clarence Williams, the Rev. Franklin Gregg (who served as principal), and Melvin Hill.

This photograph shows another graduating class from McClelland Academy, likely from around 1915. The individuals pictured are unidentified.

An early Newnan High School sports team is seen here. The Newnan mayor and city council were petitioned for the establishment of a public school system in 1874. In 1881, free schools were referred to as being one of the major needs of Newnan. The first public school building was erected in 1888 on Temple Avenue and was called the Public City School and, later, the Temple Avenue School. A larger high school building was built at the intersection of Jackson Street and Temple Avenue in 1916.

The original Newnan High School, located on Temple Avenue, was constructed in 1887–1888. For many years, this building was called the Temple Avenue School, and it later became the grammar school.

Born on December 17, 1903, in Coweta County, author Erskine Caldwell became one of the most respected and best-selling authors of the mid-20th century. His most famous and lauded works—*Tobacco Road*, *God's Little Acre*, and *You Have Seen Their Faces*—deal with themes of poverty, tenant farming, ignorance, and hopelessness in the South. This 1938 portrait of Caldwell was taken by Carl van Vechten. Caldwell wrote 12 nonfiction works, 25 novels, and about 150 short stories. His birthplace is not operated as a museum in Moreland.

Wooden bricks soaked in creosote preservative formed the streets of downtown Newnan at the turn of the 20th century. "This was the condition of the streets when we moved here," recalls Carolyn Wilson Burson in her book *Pie's Half-Baked Memoirs*. "But they were replaced sometime later with real brick because the wooden ones were ineffective with the advent of the automobile. Elizabeth Wilkinson remembered that they would swell up and burst in the hot summertime when a car ran over them."

The post office on Greenville Street was built by Algernon Blair in 1910–1911 for $47,868. The building was torn down in 1967 to make way for the new Federal Building. "Newnan's chances for securing a federal building appears promising just now," the *Newnan Weekly News* reported in 1906. "Congressman Adamson has made a favorable report of the matter to Mayor Burdett, saying that the government is prepared to take the matter under advisement. The government is prepared to spend $5,000 for a site, on which, if the building is erected, a three-story granite structure, 50 x 80 feet in size, will be placed."

This photograph shows the east side of the Newnan Court Square about 1910. "Not long ago the statement was published that Newnan is the fourth richest town, per capita, in the United States, and whether or not this is strictly accurate, it is an evident fact that the Coweta County capital is substantially prosperous," reported the *Newnan Herald and Advertiser* in 1910. "The mercantile interests are large, and the town claims several manufacturing plants of considerable magnitude."

This shows an artist's rendering of an aerial view of the city, published as a postcard by Barron's 5 & 10 Cent Store. "As a matter of fact, that is one of the finest sections of Georgia," continues an article in the *Newnan Herald and Advertiser* in 1910. "In the section surrounding Newnan are a group of progressive and hustling little towns, and the amount of improvement going on in some of them is an eye-opener."

A steel truss bridge across Line Creek was constructed on Highway 54 in 1915. The contract was won by the R.D. Cole Company, and W.J. Wood of Sharpsburg was the subcontractor. The bridge was torn down in 1947 and moved north of Wynn's Pond gristmill on Highway 54.

This photograph, taken in about 1909, shows early Newnan merchants (from left to right) J. Frank Lee, Harvey Farmer, Millard Farmer, and Pete Davis in front of a building on the East Court Square. Lee was a druggist whose business was eventually carried on by his partner, J.R. King, and his son Bill Lee at Lee-King drugstore. Farmer operated a merchandise store at the location shown here.

This photograph appears in a 1938 edition of the *Newnan Times*, announcing that it is "Cotton Picking Time in Coweta County." In the first year of the 1930s, over 15,000 bales of cotton were harvested. The first bale, ginned in 1930 by B.B. Leverett of Luthersville, weighed 520 pounds and was bought by H.C. Arnall for 12¢ per pound. By 1933, however, cotton was down to 6¢ a pound.

These colts were exhibited at the 1937 Coweta County Fair by boys in the local 4-H club. Locally, the 4-H began in 1905 as a boys' corn club in Newton County, Georgia. The Extension Service program that oversees the 4-H Club began in Coweta County in 1914, with H. Gibbs Wiley as farm demonstrator.

This shows West Washington Street in about 1885. Notice the stones in the roadway crossing for pedestrians to avoid the mud. On the right is Newnan First Baptist Church. Also pictured is the home of attorney Berryman T. Thompson, the president of McIntosh Mills and Newnan Banking Company and the state representative for Coweta County. The house was demolished to make way for a new church sanctuary.

The Cook family liked to spend time at Ray Park, off of Spring Street, like many other families in Newnan. The park, which was segregated for many years, was presented to the City of Newnan in February 1891 by Lavender Ray in honor of his father, John Ray, a pioneer citizen.

This photograph shows Greenville Street in the 1920s, when traffic on the street was still two-way and cars could be parked in the middle of the street.

The East Newnan Cotton Mill is shown here in about 1919. Cotton and textile mills brought much-needed industrial growth to the South at the turn of the 20th century. Sometimes financed by Northern industrialists wanting to take advantage of cheap labor, and other times financed locally by private stockholders to provide jobs for the landless whites, the mill system was prevalent in the South well into the mid-20th century.

The R.D. Cole Manufacturing Company was located on East Broad Street for over a century. "During the past week the R.D. Cole Manufacturing Company shipped a huge gas-producing machine to Shanghai, China, a large boiler and pneumatic tank to Korea and a boiler to Tacoma, Washington," reports a local newspaper article in 1919. "Verily, the world seems to be this company's market."

Ferries were an important part of local economic infrastructure throughout the 19th and early 20th centuries. Cable ferries like this one crossed the Chattahoochee River on the Northwest Coweta border. The cable was connected to both shores and guided the ferryboat across the water. This scene from the 1890s shows the Bowen's Ferry, and pictured are Om Coggin, on the cotton wagon; Perry Coggin, holding the lever board for the ramp; and George Coggin.

The West Court Square around 1917 is depicted in this photograph. "For the first time since the town was incorporated—over 75 years ago—Newnan passed a 'drunkless' Christmas," the *Newnan Herald* reported in 1917. "Not a single case of drunkenness was reported. More than that, if any man, white or black, had a drink concealed under his tunic he kept mighty quiet about it."

The Southern School of Telegraphy, on the South Court Square in the Reese Opera House building, is shown here. It was one of the few telegraphy schools in the country at the time.

A "cotton scene" at the Central Railroad in Newnan is seen in this photograph. The postcard notes, "W.A. Brannon in foreground on horseback." Horses, mules, and oxen provided the major means of transportation for Newnan residents for the town's first century of existence.

Early Modes of Transportation Used In Coweta

Old Coaches Of W. B. Berry Property of D.A.R.

(1) Chariot Coach. 1850-1860; 1855: (3) Victoria Carriage; (4)
(2) Express Mail Coach. 1845. Tallyho Coach.

This 1938 *Newnan Times* news story offers a look back at "Early Modes of Transportation Used in Coweta." The old coaches were the property of W.B. Berry and the Daughters of the American Revolution, and they include a "Chariot Coach" from the 1850s, an "Express Mail Coach" from 1845, a "Victoria Carriage," and a "Tallyho Coach."

Even the Newnan fire station depended on horse travel in the early years. This 1912 photograph shows Horse Company No. 1. From left to right are chief of police John Shackelford, fire chief Jim Beavers, councilman Tom Parrott, councilman Tom Goodrum, and street superintendent Bennett Sanders.

An early horse-drawn fire wagon is seen here in Newnan. At this time, the fire station was located on LaGrange Street. "The Newnan city council has been negotiating for some time with the American-La-France Fire Engine Co. of Elmira, N.Y. for the purchase of an auto fire truck for the use of the fire dept.," reports a 1915 *Newnan Herald*. "Last week the company sent one of the machines to Newnan in charge of an expert from the factory to give a demonstration of the good points claimed for it." This building currently serves as a shop and residence.

W.B. North and Polly Bridges drive a horse-drawn buggy in Coweta County in the early 1900s. The photograph was taken in Sharpsburg. It took many years for Coweta County to make the full transition to motorized vehicles.

This scene on the North Court Square is from about 1906, showing cotton farmers bringing their product to market by horse or mule. "The old street sprinkler was recommissioned yesterday in Newnan, after having come forth from the repair shop in the glory of red paint," reports a 1906 *Newnan Weekly News* article. "The high wind and dust must have been making things unpleasant in the city's business center, and the sprinkler was put into action again at an opportune time."

This photograph from about 1912 shows times were changing in Coweta County with the advent of the automobile. Taken on Standing Rock Road, the photograph shows (standing on the far left) Mary Kate Caldwell, (on the running board) Ruth Caldwell, and J.T. Caldwell. In the backseat are Mr. and Mrs. Morgan A. Caldwell. In the front seat are Wilbur (left) and George Caldwell. Standing in the back is Odessa Caldwell.

D.F. Carter (left) and John Fletcher enjoy some time in the shade after a drive in the 1920s. The *Newnan Herald and Advertiser* notes in 1909 that the "automobile craze" has taken "complete possession" of the media at the time. "The idea of having the roads of Georgia macadamized or asphalted for the pleasure of 'joy riders' who come out from the cities is too preposterous for anything. If there were no machines to be sold we dare say the craze would soon die out, and country folks could then venture upon the highways without danger to life or limb."

Rubye Sewell goes joyriding on April 13, 1930. In the early 20th century, the local newspaper criticized such "joy riders," who "disregard the US Fuel Administration's request to cooperate with the Government in conserving the supply of gasoline," saying the riders were "hereby warned that the city police have been ordered to secure the names of such slackers, and that their names will be made public."

Bill Gentry is shown here in a photograph taken on November 17, 1929. Note the rumble seat, also called the "mother-in-law seat," a popular feature at the time. The upholstered exterior seat opened from the rear deck of pre–World War II automobiles.

"Newnan's Efficient Fire Department," now motorized, is featured in a *Newnan Times* in 1938. "Local government had to keep pace with all the changes in the county," one history relates. "The city administration in Newnan had to deal with such issues as the prohibition of chickens running at large and the replacement of old boards on the sidewalk of the LaGrange Street viaduct."

An outing in Coweta County on July 4, 1928, is seen here. The Fourth of July has always been a big time of celebration in Newnan, with parades, barbecue, and other patriotic-themed events.

Boat outings were a popular form of recreation in the early 20th century at places like Pearl Lake, Lake Raymond, and the Chattahoochee River. This pastoral scene dates to the late 1920s.

Peach Season" 1928.

Seen here are "Georgia Peaches" Frances, Mildred, and Edna Cooper, a Mrs. Barnett, and Sallie, Fannie, and Allie Mae Thigpen. This photograph was taken in 1928. Coweta County heavily invested in peach production in the 1920s, growing from 42,000 trees in 1919 to 316,000 trees by the 1940s. Young Southern ladies were affectionately called "Georgia Peaches" from an early date.

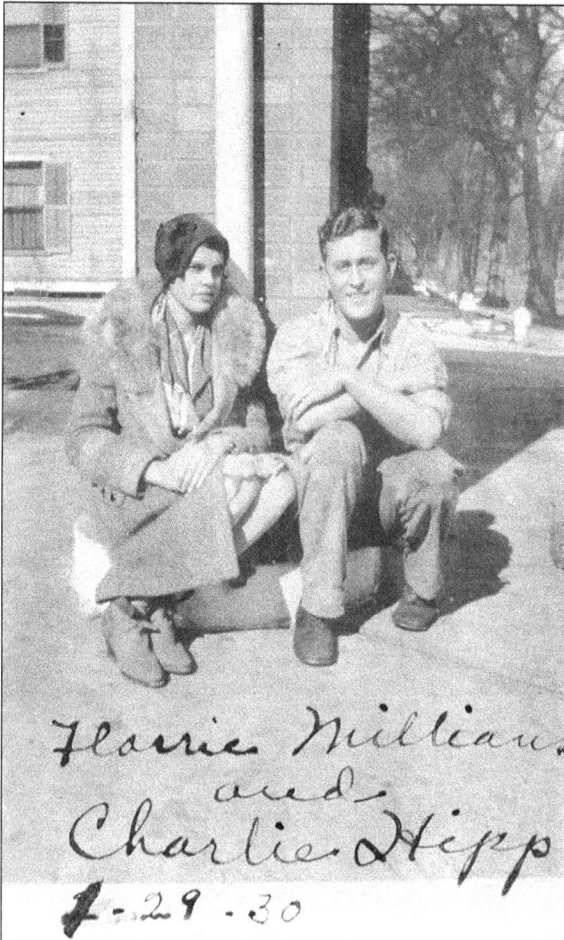

Florrie Millians and Charlie Hipp are shown here in a photograph taken on January 29, 1930, in the Welcome community. "The poor old farmer gets 'bluer' day by day as cotton prices go down," a reporter in the Welcome community said at about this time. "If they keep falling at the present rate it will take all the holdover cotton to cover insurance and storage charges." In spite of the hardships, local youth still found ways to enjoy themselves.

Traditions like Easter helped to bond a community together. Girls would often wear a new dress on Easter Sunday—for many families, this was a rare occasion to wear something new. Johnnie Millians is shown here on Easter Sunday, April 20, 1930.

Johnnie Millians

4-20-30

Easter Sunday
19-30

Isobel Copeland

Easter Sunday

Isobel Copeland is shown here on an Easter Sunday. In times of great change, holiday traditions like Easter, with its baskets, bonnets, egg hunts, and new dresses, helped families remain connected to the past.

Margaret Dukes (left) and Evelyn Millians are seen here in the late 1920s. Dukes worked for years at the Kersey's and Bruner's stores downtown.

Mayor James Brown is shown here in the 1930s. "Mayor Brown's position as head of the city's government is a reward for his fifty-three years of conscientious service in Newnan and Coweta," a 1938 *Newnan Times* reports. "He has labored cheerfully and with a right good will since coming to Newnan in 1886, and now in his eighty-fifth year. Mayor Brown combines the duties of mayor with those of United States Commissioner of the Newnan district, and at an age when most men would have retired from any form of active service, he continues to work as hard as he ever did in the interests of the people he loves so well, who return that love a thousand fold."

MAYOR JAS. E. BROWN

The Cook family in Newnan is seen in this photograph, including Romanz Cook, in the left front with bangs, with her brother and other relatives. Dick Cook's aunt Mildred Arnall Peniston wrote many letters to him while he served as a doctor in the European theater in World War II. The letters are featured at the McRitchie-Hollis Museum, at 74 Jackson Street, formerly the Peniston home. (Courtesy of the Cook family.)

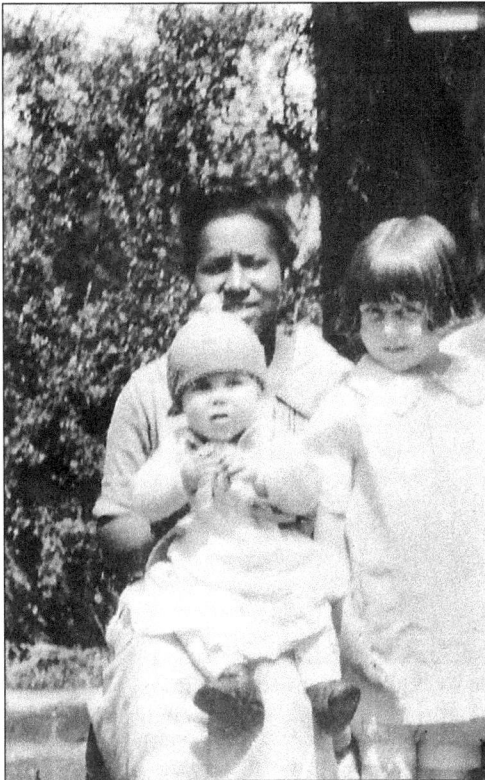

Dicky Cook, his sister Romanz Cook, and their nanny are seen here in Newnan. Overwhelmingly, people in the middle and upper classes in the South during the early-to-mid-20th century employed domestic servants to help them with cooking, cleaning, laundry, and the rearing of children. There were over two million domestic servants in the US in 1940, including 1.7 million who worked as cooks in kitchens. About 92 percent of those domestic servants were female, and more than half of them were African American. A full-time domestic servant working in the South in 1939 earned a median annual salary of $205; in Georgia, it was even lower. (Courtesy of the Cook family.)

Zipporah Kidd (left) and Mildred Martha Hodge pose for a photograph taken in about 1919. "We had a delightful time roaming through the woods and enjoyed the barbecue to the fullest extent," the classmates wrote in a memory book.

Despite their happy faces, (from left to right) Ida Sue Sewell, Myrah Sewell, and Anna C. Arnold were just as worried as the adults in their lives about World War I going on in Europe. "During the last four years events have occurred that have shaken the very foundation of civilization itself," their classmate Harold Cook Atkinson said in his valedictory speech in 1919. "This old world of ours has been stirred from center to circumference and all nations have felt the shock."

Hetty Jane Dunaway was a star of the Chautauqua show circuit in the early 20th century. Chautauqua, an adult education movement popular throughout rural America until the 1920s, was named for Chautauqua Lake, New York, where the first events were held. Chautauqua brought "culture" to rural areas that were far removed from the theater, art, and educational opportunities of big cities.

Pianist Alice Fortin (left) accompanied Wayne P. Sewell and his wife, Hetty Jane Dunaway, in their appearances on the Chautauqua circuit as they played in various towns in the 1920s and 1930s. Dunaway married Sewell and eventually moved to the Sewell family plantation in Roscoe, where she developed extensive gardens that included an amphitheater, a wishing well, fountains, and other features.

A *Trip to Japan, and Other Interesting Features* is advertised on this promotional flyer. This was one of the many shows performed by Hetty Jane Dunaway and her touring companions in the 1920s.

S. Russel Bridges, president of the Alkahest Lyceum Bureau in Atlanta, said Dunaway was "absolutely new" and of "real merit for your Lyceum or Chautauqua program." He said Dunaway had "never received an unfavorable criticism."

S. Russel Bridges
President Alkahest Lyceum Bureau
Atlanta, Georgia

IN A LETTER TO LYCEUM and CHAU-TAUQUA MANAGERS SAYS

IF you are looking for something absolutely new and of real merit for your Lyceum or Chautauqua program, engage Miss Hettie Jane Dunaway in one of her costumed musical play readings. If she fails to fill the bill, send it to me and I'll pay it.

I have booked her for the past three seasons, and have never received an unfavorable criticism. Instead, the committees usually ask for a return engagement the same season if possible. There is a reason. Miss Dunaway presents an entirely new form of entertainment—the living character readings in costume, with musical accompaniment. Besides, she is a natural artist—Southern style—looks good! She has everything in her favor and couldn't fail if she tried. I commend her most highly. For the past three seasons Miss Dunaway has presented an interpretation of "The Lady of the Decoration" with phenomenal success.

"Miss Dunaway has given to the Lyceum public a new thrill in her strikingly original and novel presentations of "The Lady of the Decoration" and "Just Plain Judy." They are new and virile productions. The atmosphere of the stories is wonderfully created, through the medium of platform accessories, beautiful costumes and special music. The stories themselves are marvelously interpreted by one born to interpret them. Beauty, pathos, humor, romance, and wholesome philosophy blend in one indescribable product which can only be appreciated by being seen and heard."

—Announcement used by the Affiliated Lyceum Bureaus of America.

Hettie Jane Dunaway

68

Wayne P. Sewell operated a farm in Roscoe and built a large barn across from the family home. The barn featured show animals such as rabbits, bears, and birds. Sewell operated Wayne P. Sewell Productions out of Atlanta, which employed a number of touring actresses and directors, most notably Sarah Ophelia Colley Cannon, later known for her character Minnie Pearl, which she developed while working for Sewell.

Wayne P. Sewell takes center stage during a large-cast production. Sewell moved his production headquarters to Dunaway Gardens in Roscoe after they were developed under the direction of his wife, Hetty Jane Dunaway. There, they trained professionals who directed plays in touring productions throughout the Southeast. Costumes for the plays were sewn at a building on Potts Road.

Hetty Jane Dunaway and her husband, Wayne P. Sewell, are shown here in *The Red Rambler*. The four-act "symbol play" featured Dunaway as "the little waif" and Sewell as "a rich man's son." "The play is a romance of rare power, deep human significance and vivid action," states a flyer from the time. The play was said to be "full of unique, humorous situations and a revelation of the human heart."

From left to right, Hetty Jane Dunaway, Wayne P. Sewell, and Marjorie Hatchett are seen here. Hatchett, Dunaway's niece, would later go on to teach theater and other subjects at Newnan High School.

This flyer reads, "Hetty Jane Dunaway and Sada San, her accompanist, in the *Lady of the Decoration*." "Miss Dunaway is so well known throughout the South and East that an introduction is hardly necessary," it states. "She has hundreds of press clippings and personal letters from all over the United States."

Virginia Miller and Edwin Strawbridge came to Dunaway Gardens in August 1940 as part of a Georgia dance festival. "Here dancers, choreographers, group directors, soloists, and technicians will meet to discuss their problems; to have the benefit of organization, discussion, and professional training," according to a contemporary news article.

The Blue Bonnet Tea Room was another popular feature of Dunaway Gardens in Roscoe.

Referred to as "The Hanging Gardens of Georgia," Dunaway Gardens was also called "the work of a lifetime." Featured at the gardens were an outdoor theater, the Hanging Gardens, the Sunken Garden, the Little Stone Mountain, a Japanese rock garden, a swimming pool, a plantation teahouse, and the Patchwork Barn Theatre. Dunaway Gardens has been fully restored and is now reopened.

A Mr. Spencer is seen here in a portrait taken at S.F. Jackson Studios in Newnan. In 1909, Jackson Studios served as the site of one of Newnan's first "moving picture shows." "We will start a moving picture show Monday night, May 24, over Holt & Cates Co.'s drug store, in the old Jackson photograph gallery," reports a *Newnan Herald and Advertiser.* "We will be open for business every night during the week from 7:30. We propose to run the highest class show that Newnan has ever had, to get the best class of pictures, to change the program every night, to have plenty of electric fans to make the place comfortable, and to run a high class, clean pace of amusement. The admission will be 5 cents."

A note on the back of this photograph reads, "Taken at Peb Arnold's place near Corinth when he had a house party." The Corinth community is located south of Newnan, just over the county line.

Eudocia Beavers, daughter of James Beavers and Elizabeth Hunter, married Confederate veteran John Hubbard Neely, son of John Hill Neely and Rebecca Whitten of Sharpsburg, on October 25, 1872, in Coweta County. Their daughter Emma Tallulah Neely, the child in this image, was born in 1874. Emma later married Walker Martin. Her siblings included Nora Addie Neely, Alma Thomas Neely, and John Robert Neely. This was taken at Jackson Studios in Newnan.

This photograph was taken at Jackson Studios in Newnan. *Coweta County Chronicles* notes that, in 1907, "S.F. Jackson, the photographer of the county for many years, died January 4."

This cabinet card photograph taken at Jackson Studios in the late 19th century features an unusual leaf border.

Jackson Studios was located over the Holt & Cates soda fountain and drugstore, where one could "go upstairs to view motion pictures for 5 cents a customer," as one local history reports. Note the long christening dress, worn by both girls and boys at the time.

Note the "Little Lord Fauntleroy" style, popular for boys' portraits at the time. Jackson Studios recorded the faces of many Newnan residents in the late 19th and early 20th centuries. However, today, many of the subjects are unidentified, and the cards have passed into the hands of the Newnan-Coweta Historical Society.

The cabinet card, very popular after 1870 up through the 1890s, consisted of a thin photograph that was mounted on a card, usually 4.25 inches by 6.5 inches. This one was taken at S.F. Jackson Studios.

Young Thompson was a local furniture maker who worked as a lathe turner. His wife, like many Newnan residents at the time, had her picture taken at Jackson & Boyd Photographers in Newnan.

This photograph was taken at Jackson Studios in the late 19th century. Note the wide knot of the tie, which was popular at the time.

This photograph of Will Black was taken at Jackson Studios in the late 19th century. It is unknown if Black was related to the Black whose name emblazons a building on Greenville Street.

This cabinet card photograph was taken at Jackson & Boyd Studios in Newnan.

Jackson & Boyd, EXTRA FINISH, NEWNAN, GA.

Note the Victorian-era props, common for photographic studios at the time, in this Jackson Studios photograph.

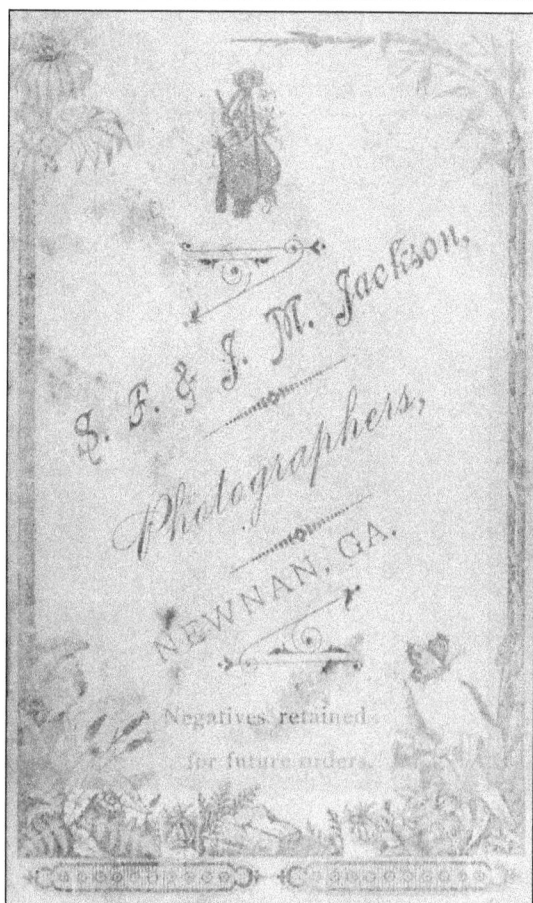

This card advertises "L.F. Hurd, Photographic Artist, Newnan GA, Studio on Hancock Street." The early business card shows a competitor of Jackson Studios.

Even though this S.F. and J.M. Jackson photography studio card states, "Negatives retained for future orders," many of the negatives from shops like these wound up in the trash heap after the businesses were sold or the original photographers passed away.

This shows a view from the 1930s of D. Mansour's Drop-In Corner, which had a dirt floor and "the best hot dogs in town," according to local resident Elizabeth Beers. The building was later remodeled to include two shops on the ground floor and office space upstairs. "Royal Crown Cola: Best By Taste Test" is promoted on the storefront.

Newnan held a parade recognizing its centennial on September 28, 1927. Arnall Mills sponsored this float, which features, from left to right, Henry C. Arnall, the grandfather of Georgia governor Ellis Arnall; his father, Joe G. Arnall; and his uncles Alton W. Arnall, H.C. Arnall Jr., and Frank M. Arnall.

The Newnan High School class of 1904 includes, from left to right (first row) John Robinson, Willis J. Davis, and Earl Chandler; (second row) Lorenna Robertson (far left) and Annie Lizzie Widener (far right); (third row) Yasabel Salbide, Christine Cole, Sallie Frances Mann, Margaret Summers, and Cammie Daniel; (fourth row) Nell Pinson, Nannaline King, Katie Sue Brewster, Bennetta Orr, and Annie Mae Robertson.

The second Newnan High School building is shown here, on the lot bounded by Temple Avenue and Jackson Street.

Little girls loved their dolls, even a century ago. These appear to be German-made Kestner bisque dolls, popular in the late 19th and early 20th centuries.

A Newnan High School honor roll program booklet from 1910–1911 is shown here.

The Newnan City Schools

Commencement Exercises

Monday, May 29th, 1911, at 3 p. m.

ORATORICAL CONTEST

AUDITORIUM

Music	Astin's Orchestra
The Little Boy Who Ran Away	John Pendergrast
The Night Wind	Helen Dent
A School Girl's Trial	Tommie Martin
Waltz, Piano Solo	Dorothy Leach
Dead Pussy Cat	Sarah Askew
Belshazzar's Feast	James Brewster
The Little Friend In The Mirror	Martha Burns
Song by First and Second Grades of Atkinson Grammar School	
His Prompt Obedience	Mary Hamrick
High Tide at Gettysburg	Emory Murray
The Speckled Hen	Elizabeth North
Lazingana	Miss Mae Payne
The Bachelor's Sale	Alma Holeman
The Soldier Tramp	Jewel Webb
Two Little Rogues	Jennie Fowler
Song by Second and Third Grades of Atkinson Grammar School	
The Dead Doll	Frances Glover
Nathan Hall,	Thomas Cole
So Was I.	Janie Lee Johnson
Sleep, My Dolly	Nona Stephens

Medal presented by Col. T. G. Farmer and Col. Alvan H. Freeman.

This is a program from the commencement exercises of Newnan City Schools on Monday, May 29, 1911. Participants in the program included John Pendergrast, Helen Dent, Tommie Martin, Dorothy Leach, Sarah Askew, James Brewster, Martha Burns, Mary Hamrick, Emory Murray, Elizabeth North, May Payne, Alma Holeman, Jewel Webb, Jennie Fowler, Frances Glover, Thomas Cole, Janie Lee Johnson, and Nona Stephens. Recognition medals were presented by local merchants T.G. Farmer and Alvan H. Freeman.

Five

WORLD WAR II

By October 1940, about 3,000 Coweta County men had registered for the national draft. A total of 63 died in service. The men pictured here were inducted into the Army on July 8, 1943. They are shown here as they ready to board the train to Fort McPherson in Atlanta. Included in this group are, among others, Johnny Powell, Morgan Hopson, P.F. Musick, Haygood Justiss, and William N. Banks.

Lt. Robert "Bobby" Beers, shown here during his service with the Army Air Corps, was the youngest of five sons in the Beers family, and the only one to be killed in action. When he died, on August 11, 1942, he was the first known war casualty from Coweta County. (Courtesy of Elizabeth Beers.)

Coweta families often learned of loved ones killed in war through an official telegram such as this one. "Deeply regret to inform you" were not the words any family wished to hear.

The local Woolworth's store displayed photographs of local servicemen in its windows. Passersby would know a man was killed in action when a blue silk square with a gold star was placed over the photograph. Local newspapers regularly published Local Men in Service to keep the community informed. Pictured is Bobby Beers, who died in an airplane accident in England. (Courtesy of Elizabeth Beers.)

Mildred Arnall Peniston, wife of Arnall Mills president Ellis Peniston, lived at 74 Jackson Street during World War II and wrote frequent letters to her nephews serving in the war. "Am sitting by the radio waiting for the Official Announcement that war in Germany is over and that this is VE Day," wrote Peniston to Capt. Dick Cook in 1945. "Am ready for my boys to come on back and be with their families." The letters are on display at the McRitchie-Hollis Museum in Newnan.

R. E. BEERS

MRS. E. H. PENISTON
74 JACKSON STREET
NEWNAN, GEORGIA

Monday
April 9, 1945.

Dearest Dick,
    Just a little note to le
you know that I am thinking
of you.
    Penny came down and spe
F___d. with us. He left early

Families of workers at Southern Mills in Senoia are gathered for this photograph in 1942. Many local industries shifted to war production during the 1940s, and women often entered the workforce for the first time. This photograph includes, in no particular order, Charles Welden, Dorothy Welden, Lloyd Bell, Ava Nell Bell, Leon Shell, Ida Mae Adcock, Edwin Cheek, a Mr. Brand, Pete Clark, Dorothy Clark, Frank Clark, John Byram, James Byram, Cecil Hardy, Virginia Shell, Willie Banks, Leon Cavender, Lucy Cavender, Roy Shell, Ethel Shell, James Glazier, Geraldine Glazier, J.T. Barnette, Mr. Pratlin, Hamilton Arnold, a Mr. Ellis, M.E. Thompson, a Mrs. Thompson, Ruth Byram, Jim Lykins, a Mr. Bird, a Mr. Busby, Bob Howard, J.D. Johnson, Jim Grey, a Mr. Howard, Willard Kierbow, Ralph Putnam, George Caldwell, Vara Caldwell, Mrs. Maddox, Edna Johnson, Hazel Nixon, Pauline Arnold, Melvin Cheek, Julia Roberts, and Aubrey Williams.

Fourteen Carloads For Defense

Rrom Newnan to Uncle Sam, with best wishes went these 14 carloads for defense. Shown Friday as they were inspected by E. G. Cole and B. M. Blackburn, R. D. Cole executives, before shipment, the cars contain 17 giant bell-buoys for the U. S. Coast Guard. Took four months to build 'em.

Like many local industries, the R.D. Cole Manufacturing Company shifted to war production during World War II, becoming one of three steel fabricators that made mast posts for Liberty ships. The company also made stanchions, king posts, deck equipment, and steel ocean buoys. In 1943, the wartime production of R.D. Cole was recognized by the United States Maritime Commission and Cole employees were presented with a Victory Fleet flag and individual merit badges.

In War Theatre

WENDELL ADAMS is
among many Newnanites
in the Pacific theatre

Wendell Adams was among the earliest "local boys" featured on the front pages of the *Newnan Times* and the *Newnan Herald* during World War II. Adams served in the Pacific theater.

Newnan Cotton Mills, founded in 1888, received the Army-Navy Award for Excellence in War Production in March 1943. The "E" award ("Emblem for Excellence") included a pennant to be flown over the plant and a lapel pin for each employee. This photograph includes, in no particular order, Robert Cannon, Henry Quick, Nell Harrison, Modena Thrower, Pearl Ward, Minnie Long, Kella Watts, Vara Chappell Brazee, Irene Sewell, Iula Morris, Ruth Thomas, Lizzie Cole, Charlie Horton, R.T. Stanford, Lessie Embry, Gladys Black, Bill Borders, Zuma Knott, Raymond Garner, Belle Pounds, Norma Bailey, Eula Rice, Minnie Hudson, Tack Herring, Ethel Dean, Sally Reese, Aurey Shellnut, Mae Hembrick, Orrie Smith, Lurie Olmstead, Lizzie Story, Pearl Olmstead, Beulah Dearman, Etoy Harrison, Tharra Gordon, Lois Quick Ozmore, Clyde Duffy, Florence Williams, Walter Ayers, Otis Gray, Ed Ozmore, Charlie Hines, Luther Smith, Gus Black, Cecil Williams, Bustiner Witherinton, Mr. Carroll, Curtis Duffey, Jack Rooks, Mercer Gordon, Jack Ward, Byron Harrison, Alec Long, Roscoe Williams, James Parks, Dan Rice, Lee Williamson, Bernard Evans, Reese Newell, Jim Holman, Aubrey Shellnut, Lester Melear, George Kelly, Marvin Dearman, Clint Hubbard, Minor Thrower, Jay Estep, Trent Kelly, A.J. Bailey, J.J. Duffy, Jim Brown, Kirk Horsley, Richard Long, Fletch McWhorter, and C.B. Knott.

The Newnan Herald

A Good Weekly Newspaper

RNALL ASSURED OF GOVERNORSHIP 2:00 A.M. UNOFFICIAL RETURNS

Evans, Carmical 'In' As Commissioners

ELLIS ARNALL

"There's nothing wrong with government that a little democracy won't cure," said Ellis Arnall of Newnan, Georgia's World War II governor. Arnall (1907–1992) was born in a house on Wesley Street to a prominent textile-mercantile family, and he grew up to become one of Georgia's most progressive governors. Arnall established the board of regents, restored accreditation to the state university system, led efforts to lower the voting age to 18, eliminated the poll tax, reformed the state prison system, established a merit pay system for state employees, and adopted a new state constitution. He also led a court challenge to reduce discriminatory freight rates that stood in the way of the South's economic development.

"What's it good for?" "Guns, tanks, and maybe part of a plane." The local newspapers participated in massive propaganda efforts to inspire patriotism, promote conservation of resources, and invite local people to participate in the war effort.

JUNK
needed for War

"What's it good for?"
"Guns, tanks, and maybe part of a plane"

In the attics and cellars of homes, in garages, tool sheds, and on farms, is a lot of Junk which is doing no good where it is, but which is needed at once to promptly, the full rate of production cannot be attained or increased; the necessary tanks, guns, and ships cannot be produced.

The rubber situation is also critical. In spite of the recent rubber drive, there is

JUNK MAKES FIGHTING WEAPONS

One old radiator will provide

Virginia Trammell Jarrard of Moreland holds her infant son Tom in 1943 at the home of her parents, Mr. and Mrs. Robert Toombs. Like many wives whose husbands were fighting overseas, Jarrard lived with her parents during the war.

Comdr. Paul "Penny" Cook received the Navy Cross and two Distinguished Flying Crosses during his service in World War II. Cook was involved in the rescue mission of future president George H.W. Bush after the plane Bush was piloting was shot down over the Pacific. (Courtesy of the Cook family.)

This photograph, taken in April 1943 at the Newnan depot, shows a group of local men newly inducted into the service and readying for their deployment. Kneeling in front are Sanford Pike of Newnan (left) and Harold Burnham of Sargent. The two standing on the far left are John Henry Mobley and Buren Borders, both from Arnco. Second from the right, wearing a hat, is Reuben Smith of Arnco.

Stanley Brittain, a battery plant worker, served in the Navy during World War II. Brittain was born in Sharpsburg and attended Starr High School.

This photograph, taken in 1942, shows the third-grade class of the old Murray Street School. From left to right are, (first row) Jo Ann Hubbard, Shirley Duffey, Florence Rice, Iris Harrison, Betty Hamby, Francis McAfee, and unidentified; (second row) Wilson Bernhard, Kenneth Parks, Bobby Thomas, Cary Duncan, Bobby Dearman, Emmett Long, Tom Hall, and Roy Hendrix; (third row) Bobby Olmestead, Elmer Newell, Raymond Garner, Joe Walls, Reginald Duncan, Byron Griffith, Quinton Thrower, and Billy Moat; (fourth row) Douglas Kelly, Gibbs Mobley, unidentified, Joe Scarbough, Jimmy Gordon, and Barry Ayres.

This photograph was taken in 1943 at 209 Jackson Street, the home of the Arnall family, on the occasion of Alvan Arnall's birthday. Alvan was the son of Gov. Ellis Arnall and his wife, Mildred Slemons Arnall. From left to right are (first row) Malcolm H. "Chip" Cole Jr., Richard Hubbard, Walker Johnson, Peggy Perryman Thompson, Alvan Arnall, unidentified, unidentified, and John Perryman; (second row) unidentified, Guy Arnall, unidentified, unidentified, and Parks Cole; (third row) Carolyn Kirby, Nan Young, Virginia Moody, ? Askew, Ivan Allen III, and Inman Allen.

Shown at Clearwater Lake in 1942 are, from left to right, Florence Polk Robertson, Henry and May Palmer, Goodman Robertson, George Robertson, and Jim Robertson. The Robertsons were from Turin, where Florence was a teacher for many years.

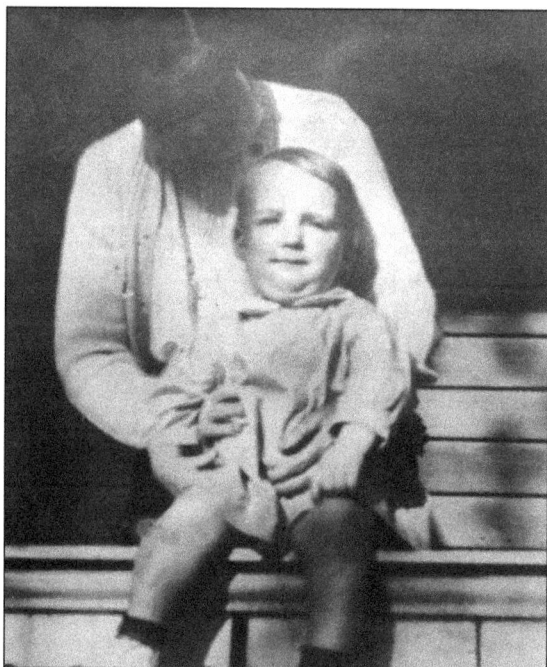

Nellie Trammell enjoys a moment in about 1940 on the front porch of her home, located between Moreland and Luthersville, with her nephew Bob Trammell. Nellie was a longtime clerk at the Moreland Mills.

The Howard Warner School took this photograph of its newest students in 1945. These are the students who moved from the seventh to the eighth grade that year, after leaving Ruth Hill Elementary School. The old school building was located on Savannah Street. The group includes, from left to right, (first row) Claude McGee, Clarence Bohannon, Edward North, unidentified, unidentified, Harold Neely, Alonzia Houston, and Clarence Freeman; (second row) Nancy Dyer, Miriam Jackson, Elma Smith, Everlena Power, unidentified, unidentified, Gussie Alexander, Ollie Lee Goolsby, Virginia Neely, and Annie Brown; (third row) unidentified, unidentified, unidentified, Martha Jean Berry, unidentified, Susie Redwine, unidentified, Elnora ?, Martha Kate Thurman, and the teacher. No one in the fourth row is identified.

This 1946 graduating class at the Howard Warner High School was the first class of professor F.A. Dodson. Shown, from left to right, are (first row) Eunice Woods, Rosa M. Arnold, Isiah Hollins, Hattie Jordan, Pollie F. Smith, Evelyn Arnold, Margaret R. Mitchell, Gladys Pittman, and Odessa R. Ragland; (second row) Gertrude N. Smith, Carolyn M. Reese, Ruby C. Lynch, Annie M. Morgan, Leona Levell, Vertelle Jordan, Katie Reeves, and Muriel Ransby; (third row) Pauline Marsh, Lillian Herring, Flossie D. Arnold, Ruth Simmons Gay, Alonza Walthal, Mary F. Herndon, Christeen North, Helen Reed, and Henrietta Johnson; (fourth row) Martha Jones Smith, Alice L. Rosser, Willie M. Pittman, Doris Price, Sarah C. Smith, Garvin Arnold, Jimmie Hunter, Gracie Coleman, Eva K. Smith, Hugh Harden, and Florene Walker.

The "Temple Avenue Boogers" of the 1940s engaged in pranks like putting acorns in their parents' gas tanks, but they also spent time playing and caroling together when they were not up to some kind of mischief, according to Sarah Jane Burson. The Boogers include, from left to right, Jan Davis, Bobby Burson, Letitia Sanders Downing, Melissa Sanders Thomas, and Joe Burson.

A group of women at Central Baptist Church formed the Sarah Hall Ladies' Missionary Society in 1940, when this photograph was taken. This photograph of the society includes, in no particular order, Mrs. W.Y. Barnes, Mrs. H.C. Glover, Mrs. Bob Farmer, Mrs. Karl Nixon, Ethel Smith, Mrs. Roy Cole, Mrs. Harold Sewell, Mrs. Harold Sewell, Mrs. T.M. Sewell, Mrs. Tom Dixon, Mrs. Pat Yancey, Mrs. George Dean, Mrs. Robert Alexander, Mrs. Glenn Ware, Mattie Reid Robinson, Mrs. Alvan Freeman, Mrs. Dick Combee, Mrs. Hamilton Arnall, Mrs. C.B. Glover, Mrs. Howard Glover, Mrs. Will Perry, Mrs. A.J. Jones, Mrs. N.B. Hudson, Mrs. N.L. North, Mrs. G.W. Jackson, Mrs. Willie Stephens, Mrs. Emil Mann, Hattie Whitaker, Mrs. Hugh Farmer, Mrs. N.V. Davis, Mrs. Fred Scisson, Mrs. Charlie Barron, Mrs. Guy Cole, Mildred Caldwell, Mrs. Rufus Askew, Mrs. Linwood Beers, Helen Long, Mrs. F.K. Underwood, Mrs. H.D. Walker, Mrs. Frank Lee, Mrs. Charlie Farmer, Mrs. Raleigh Arnall, Mrs. Thad Buchanan, Frances Glover, Mrs. Herman Glass, Mrs. R.H. McDonald, Mrs. L.S. Sewell, Ximena Strong, Mrs. Jerome Jay, Mrs. Herbert McKoy, and Mrs. S.H. Parker.

This photograph shows a family outing at Lake Raymond in 1941 on what was reportedly the first speedboat in Coweta County, a Garwood motorboat. In the boat are, from left to right, Joe Carrasco, Alice Carrasco, Joe Carassco Jr., Dr. E.P. Carrasco, Effie Carrasco La Fargue, Totsie Carrasco McKnight, and Margaret Billingsley.

Future Newnan-Coweta Historical Society president Bill Miller relaxes for a moment in the Philippines during his tour of duty there in World War II. Miller later married Coweta native Miriam Camp, moved to Moreland, and became mayor of the town.

Guy Cole is shown here in his office at the R.D. Cole Manufacturing Company during World War II. R.D. Cole was for many years Newnan's oldest industry. It was bought by an Illinois company in 1968 and eventually sold to Brown Steel. R.D. Cole was known for its decorative woodwork and bargeboard, which were used extensively in homes of this area. In later years, the company was known for its elevated water tanks, including the tank on Bullsboro Drive.

Born in Newnan on July 29, 1923, Howard Augustus McNeil Jr. served in the Navy during World War II. He enlisted at the US Naval Air Base in Atlanta on October 13, 1942. His father, Rev. Howard A. McNeil, was a Methodist minister who married Bessie Orelia Brittain of Coweta County. This photograph was taken while McNeil was stationed at a training station in Morehead, Kentucky.

Before it was Hutchinson Hardware, this building on Main Street in Senoia was home to the Hutchinson Motor Company. The Ford dealership, owned by J.B. Hutchinson, was operated from 1928 to 1947. During World War II, civilian automobiles were generally unavailable, so Hutchinson began operating a hardware store there in 1942. The store was operated at the same location, and by the same family, for decades. Longtime owner Jimmy Hutchinson recalled that cars and trucks would be delivered one at a time by drivers, usually at night, rather than by large truck delivery.

These sisters from Coweta County are seen while visiting their uncle Alonzo Bailey in Dayton, Ohio, in about 1942. At left is Marion Bailey, and at right is Evelyn Bailey Coleman. The sisters grew up in Raymond, southeast of Newnan on Highway 16. Marion later moved to Atlanta, while Evelyn moved to Chattanooga. The Sheddens, who developed the community of Raymond in the early 1900s, had employed the sisters' father, Will Bailey, at their large summer home, called the Bungalow. Bailey worked as an overseer at the Bungalow, as well as a carpenter, chauffeur, and rent collector.

This photograph shows the jail in Greenville, Georgia, where sharecropper William "Wilson" Turner spent his final days before his life ended in a car chase that took him to Moreland, past the Coweta-Meriwether county line. Turner's murder, by the politically connected John Wallace, and the resulting trial at the Coweta County Courthouse was a media sensation in 1948, leading to a best-selling book by Margaret Anne Barnes and a television movie starring Andy Griffith and Johnny Cash.

COWETA COUNTY JAIL
NEWNAN GA

Murder suspect John Wallace was kept in a cell at the old county jail in downtown Newnan, facing East Broad Street. An April 29, 1948, edition of the *Newnan Times-Herald* wryly describes Wallace as a "guest" of Sheriff Lamar Potts. The Spanish Mission–style jail was constructed in 1911 by the Georgia Construction Company and torn down in 1986 to make way for what is now the County Administration Building. C. Lloyd Preacher of Augusta was the architect and engineer. "The new jail building was formally turned over to the County Commissioners on Nov. 22 by the contractors and Jailor West is as proud of his new domicile as a boy with his first pair of boots," reports a 1911 *Newnan Herald and Advertiser*. "It is a model county prison in every respect, and as attractive architecturally as it is up to date in its equipment." The old county jail was a casualty of county expansion, said commissioner Leroy Johnson. "The old jail sat on the east side, in a building on the corner," said Johnson. "We had to tear it down. But we had some folks that didn't want to tear down the old jail. They wanted to keep it as a marker. But we just couldn't do it. It was in the way." The board had a called meeting and decided to start taking down the old jail at 1:00 a.m. "By 7 a.m., it would be gone," he said. "If we had tried to do that during the day time, half of Newnan would be there trying to stop it. I did get a couple of calls about it, but not too much."

Lamar Potts became Coweta County sheriff in 1937 and served in that office for decades. He is famously portrayed by Johnny Cash in the television movie *Murder in Coweta County*, which tells the story of what is probably Potts's most famous case, the investigation and arrest of murderer John Wallace. "Sheriff Potts has the reputation of being one of the most outstanding law enforcement officers in the state of Georgia," the *Times-Herald* newspaper reports in its centennial publication from 1965. "He is widely known for his ability to solve criminal cases."

Six

THE CITY OF HOMES

The Dent-Ballard Home, on Temple Avenue, was built in 1852. Judge W.B.W. Dent owned about 60,000 acres of land. This lot is surrounded by dogwood, oak, and pecan trees. Like many local homes, the Dent residence was used as a hospital during the Civil War.

Local preservationist Georgia Shapiro was instrumental in preserving the old Male Academy in the 1970s, when this photograph was taken. "Something came on the market that piqued our interest," said Shapiro, recalling a time she had been house hunting in Newnan in the 1970s. A building on College Street just "didn't make sense." "I stood on the sidewalk looking at it, and it had a row of windows going down the side. That wasn't like any house in town that I'd ever seen. I remember thinking to myself that this wasn't a house, this was something else." Not long afterward, Shapiro was thumbing through the *Newnan Times-Herald*'s centennial book when she was struck by an old photograph. "There it was," she said. "This was the same building I had seen on College Street. I was dumbfounded." She got into her car and raced to the building. "I counted windows. I checked their position and size. I counted the boards, from the base of the building to the window. There was absolutely no doubt about it." What she discovered was the long-lost Male Academy building, a 19th-century Newnan school for boys. Eventually, the city found money for the project, and the building was relocated to its current site at the corner of College Street and Temple Avenue, where it serves as the home of the Newnan-Coweta Historical Society. This spot was close to what was thought at the time to have been the building's original location.

The Glover home, at 45 College Street, is seen here. Howard Clarke Glover was born in Wilcox County, Alabama, on August 2, 1870. He went to school in Newnan under Professors Moses, Walker, and Pendergrast and enrolled at Auburn University, but he had to return home because of his father's ill health, according to the *History of Coweta County, Georgia*. He became a merchant along with his brother Clifford Banks Glover and married Fannie Virginia Jones at Central Baptist Church in 1898. The five-bedroom, 6,000-square-foot home was built in 1923.

The old police station at the Coweta County Courthouse was in operation from 1946 to 1959. The building has since been torn down. It was located on the southeast corner of the courthouse.

Ellis Mansour's was "one of the largest and most fascinating" department stores on the Newnan Court Square, according to Carolyn Wilson Burson. "The allure of Mansour's will never be duplicated, for you could go in and browse to your heart's content . . . There was a special redolence about the store that I miss; maybe it was from the overalls and Levis stacked on tables according to size. Whatever it was, the store was mighty popular."

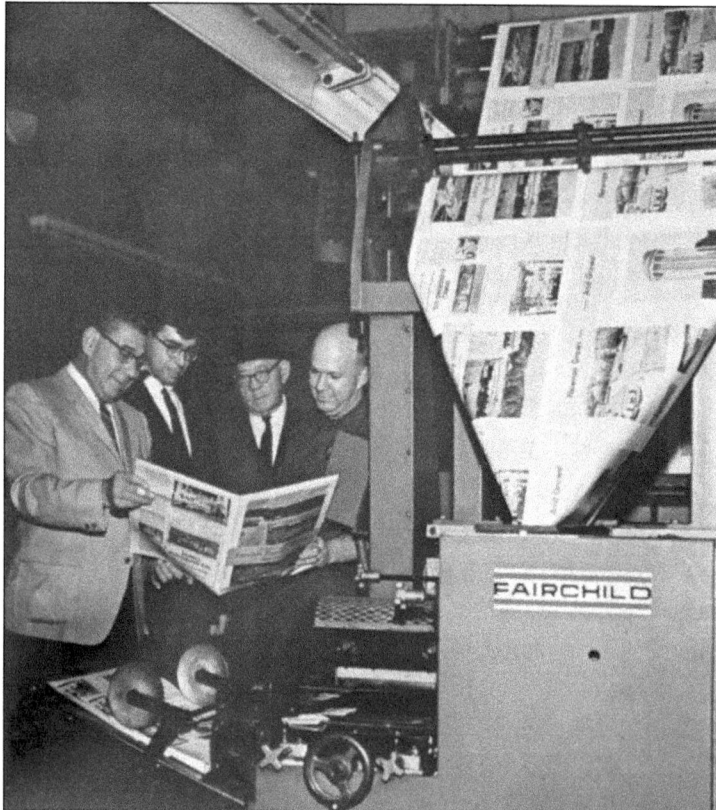

The 1965 centennial edition of the *Newnan Times-Herald* celebrated a century of publication by the local newspaper, which put out its first edition on Saturday, September 9, 1865, when "all the type was set by hand, and the paper was printed on a hand-fed press," as writers noted. Pictured from left to right are James Thomasson, managing editor at the time; Billy Thomasson, assistant to the publishers; Evan W. Thomasson, editor; and Bill Mitchum, pressman, as the latest issues comes off of a Fairchild News King offset press.

Mansour's and McConnell's stores are shown here on the North Court Square. "When I was a child, 'Ten Cent' stores were popular and seemed to be on every side of the Court Square," recalls Carolyn Wilson Burson. "McCrory's was on the West, McConnell's on the North, and Kessler's and Woolworth's on the East." The Mansour's building, remodeled to include two shops on the ground floor and office space upstairs, now houses Genelle's beauty shop.

The Gem Theatre was one of two movie theaters operating on the West Court Square, along with the Alamo. The Gem was located at 22 Court Square. The 241-seat theater dated back to the silent era and was renovated in the 1930s by Lam Amusements. The theater was smaller than the Alamo and featured many B movies on Saturdays. It closed in about 1950. "I remember it well," recalled Jack Brannon. "It didn't have a balcony like the Alamo did. I think it cost seven cents and the Alamo was 10 cents, but later raised the price to 12 cents when the Gem closed." Carolyn Wilson Burson remembered, "At least once or twice a week the movie would go off . . . the picture would just disappear, leaving the screen a complete blank."

Lee-King was the major downtown drugstore on the Newnan Square for most of the 20th century. "And they had a place there where you could get sandwiches and soups," Leroy Johnson recalled. Carolyn Wilson Burson remembered, "Some of the drug stores closed their lunch counters when integration came along in the sixties, but not Lee-King, they continued to serve their delicious sandwiches and soups and the same kinds of milk shakes and banana splits they had been serving for years, and anyone would be welcome, no matter the color of their skin." The Lee-King Drug Company is still fondly remembered for its chicken salad plate, grilled cheese sandwiches, chocolate milk shakes, cherry Coca-Colas, and egg salad sandwiches. The last of the downtown drugstores, it closed its doors in 1998. It now operates in a new location away from the Court Square. (Both, courtesy of Elizabeth Beers.)

Brothers Ltd. was another store operated for decades by the Mansour family on the Court Square in Newnan. "The Mansour name is still synonymous with the word 'merchant,'" said Carolyn Wilson Burson. The popular apparel shop "helped revitalize the Court Square," she said. (Courtesy of Elizabeth Beers.)

Hartman's and Cato's are shown here on the North Court Square. Chain clothing stores have moved out to Bullsboro Drive and Ashley Park in more recent years, and the Court Square now features more locally owned restaurants and specialty shops. (Courtesy of Elizabeth Beers.)

Kersey's and United Department Store were once located on the Court Square. "Kersey and Prather was a popular store that sold men's and women's ready-to-wear," recalled Carolyn Wilson Burson. The proprietors also sold cosmetics, perfume, and skin powders. "There was a little alcove in the back of the store where every size, shape and color of ladies' hats were displayed." (Courtesy of Elizabeth Beers.)

Connally Rexall Drugs was located for many years on the East Court Square. It was one of many drugstores that used to populate the downtown area, none of which remain today. The last drugstore on the Court Square closed in 1998. (Courtesy of Elizabeth Beers.)

Belk-Gallant is shown here, flanked by Brothers Ltd. on the north and Lee-King drugs to the south. Belk later relocated to a shopping center on Bullsboro Drive, then to another, larger shopping center near Interstate 85, and, finally, to the Newnan Crossing Bypass road, adjacent to Ashley Park. (Courtesy of Elizabeth Beers.)

Kessler's and Connally Drugs are shown here on the East Court Square, now the location of Golden's Restaurant. "I can still smell the 'just popped' popcorn and the fresh nuts that Kessler's sold in bulk," recalled Carolyn Wilson Burson. Z.P. Barron was the manager, and Bernice Stamps and Edna Wood worked as clerks at the store. "My family shopped at Kessler's a lot because most of their merchandise was priced in line with our family income, very low!" Burson said. Most purchases were made with cash, which was placed in a vacuum tube to the main office for processing. (Courtesy of Elizabeth Beers.)

Diana Shops was once a popular chain of dress stores with locations throughout the Southeast, carrying various lines of dresses, coats, suits, sportswear, bathing suits, and evening wear. (Courtesy of Elizabeth Beers.)

Bruner's Women's Wear, Lee-King drugs, Ragland Hardware Company, and Dixie Loans are shown here on the Newnan Court Square in the mid-1960s. (Courtesy of Elizabeth Beers.)

R.S. Mann Jewelers and Cavender's shop are shown on Greenville Street. Ray DuBose still operates the family jewelry business in the same building. (Courtesy of Elizabeth Beers.)

A prime example of the extravagant millwork for which the R.D. Cole Company was so famous can be seen at the Parrott-Camp-Soucy Home on Greenville Street. Featured in the 2012 film *The Odd Life of Timothy Green*, the home was originally constructed in the 1840s by William Nimmons, but was totally transformed and victorianized by owner Charles Parrott in 1890 at a cost of approximately $10,000. The 5,000-square-foot home was carefully restored by Charles and Sam Soucy in 1984. The home is one of the most unique structures in Newnan.

Kermit Hunter (1910–2001) was known for his outdoor dramas, most famously for *Unto These Hills*, a version of which still plays annually in Cherokee, North Carolina. One of his plays told the story of the life and death of Chief William McIntosh. At one time, there was talk of commissioning Hunter to write a play for the Dunaway Gardens amphitheater, but it never came to fruition.

The Princess and the Swineherd was presented by the local theater company on June 12, 1971. The princess is portrayed by Judy Gillian. The ladies in waiting are, from left to right, Wanda Giudici, Elizabeth Schuett, and Betty Jane Peppers.

The wishing well at Dunaway Gardens in Roscoe was overgrown, just like the rest of the gardens, by the 1990s.

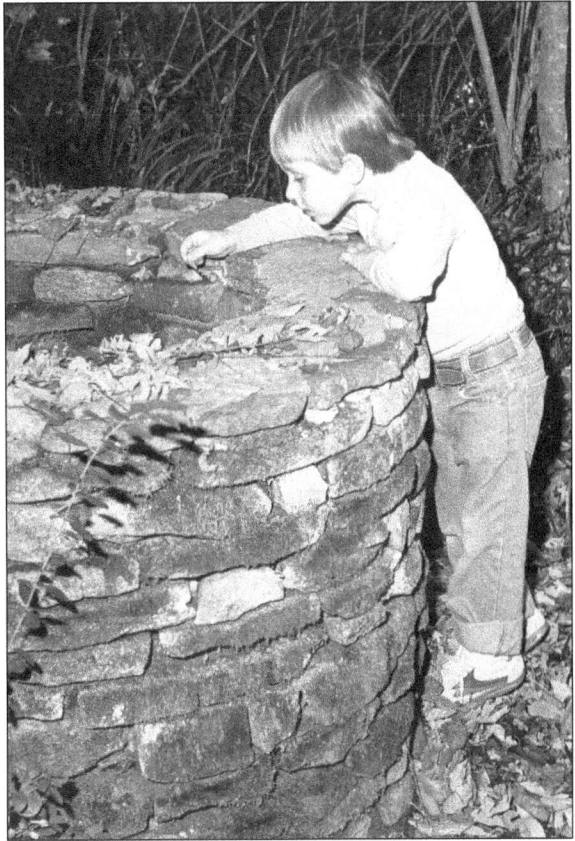

The old Dunaway Gardens amphitheater in Roscoe was still largely intact, though overgrown, by the mid-1990s, prior to the purchase and restoration of the gardens.

Longtime Coweta County Commissioner Leroy Johnson recalled in 2010 that a young man from the Corinth Road area came to see him in the 1960s, telling him that his grandfather was involved in building the courthouse, and that he would like to plant a white oak tree there in his memory. "So we set it out on the south side and had a little ceremony," said Johnson. "It grew to be a pretty good shade tree. You know those white oaks are just beautiful trees. And wouldn't you know it, that was one of the first ones they took down" when the renovations began about five years ago, he said. "Of course I know those were old trees and they were spending a lot of money on them," he said. "I know those magnolias can be pretty nasty trees to deal with."

Lead public health nurse Alice Jackson is seen here at the new health department on Jackson Street in the early 1990s. The health department had previously been located on Perry Street. Several years ago, the Coweta County Health Department building moved again, this time to a new facility on Hospital Road.

W.C. Adamson, who served for many years on the Coweta County Commission, was a descendant of some of the earliest Coweta pioneer families. "Coweta County was settled by farming people largely from South Carolina," Adamson wrote in 1965. "The people were from many classes financially, some wealthy slave owners and many working people with no slaves . . . There are some people who think agriculture is sick or dying in Georgia and Coweta County. They have always been proven wrong."

Wilbon Clay and Leroy Johnson served together on the Coweta County Commission in the early 1990s. Johnson, from Turin, represented the eastern section of the county for 38 years. He became a county commissioner on September 8, 1954, on his 38th birthday. Johnson took the same seat his father had held until his death. "The county commissioners met in the northwest corner of the courthouse," he said. "We had two rooms, and there was a table in the center of the main room, and back behind it was a small room where we kept the safe."

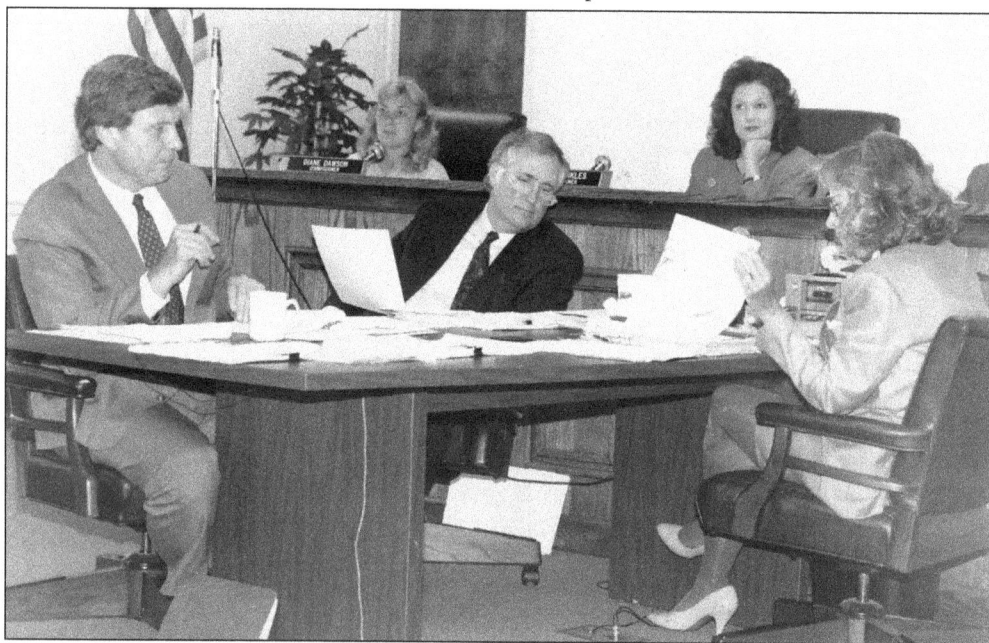

Seen here from left to right are county attorney Mitch Powell, county commissioner Diane Dawson, county administrator Richard Bray, commission chair Vicki Winkles, and county clerk Phyllis Owens. Winkles and Dawson were the first women elected to serve on the Coweta County Commission, and Winkles was the first female chair of the board. Powell later went on to serve on the Coweta County Board of Education as its chairman. The local library is named in his honor.

Wilbon Clay and Audrey Bray are shown here at a local meeting. Clay was the first African American elected county commissioner in Coweta County and the first black person to hold any countywide elected office. He also served as chairman of the board in the early 1990s. Audrey Marie Hennen Bray, a civic leader and longtime congressional aide, operated the Newnan Bakery on West Washington Street for 14 years. She became friends with Newt Gingrich, a West Georgia College professor who ran for Congress twice before being elected in 1978. When he took office, he hired Bray to work in his local office. She also later worked for Rep. Mac Collins.

William W. Williams (left) and Mike Barber are seen here. Williams served as the first chairman of the Coweta County Development Authority and the similarly named Development Authority of Coweta County, which overlaps in some of its board membership but has different powers. Williams served as chairman of both boards for decades, until the early 1990s, when the chairmanship passed to local bank president Barber.

The biggest trouble with the Coweta County Courthouse in the early-to-mid-20th-century was finding a place to park, said Leroy Johnson, "Especially when they had court." Johnson said that, despite the recent loss of the trees around the building, it is hard to argue with the recent renovations. The courthouse now looks better than ever, he said: "Just driving by, it looks real nice."

Located at 60 East Broad Street, the Newnan Historic Depot (Newnan History Center) was originally constructed as a freight and passenger depot for the Atlanta & West Point Railroad in the 1850s. The depot was the site of an encounter between Federal and Confederate forces in July 1864. As a raiding party of Federal troops approached from the east, it was surprised at the depot by Confederate troops who had been detained by rail damage north of Newnan at Palmetto. A brief skirmish ensued, followed by a two-day pitched battle south of Newnan at Brown's Mill on Corinth Road, which ended in a victory for the Confederates.

After passenger and freight train service was discontinued at the Newnan depot in the 1950s, the former depot briefly served as a seed store before the building fell into disrepair. Subsequently, the passenger section and freight platform were torn down. In the mid-1990s, the remaining portion of the building was donated to the Newnan-Coweta Historical Society. In 2000, with renewed interest in the Battle of Brown's Mill, a plan was formulated to commemorate the Corinth Road site and use the depot as an educational facility. The society, with the support and efforts of local representative Lynn Smith, received a grant from the governor's office to restore the building.

The Atkinson-Glover Home, located at 19 Temple Avenue, was designed in the Queen Anne style by architect J.W. Golucke and built in 1895 by T.E. Atkinson. The asymmetrical home features a tower on the left and a gazebo porch on the right. Balconies, bays, arches, and dormers enliven the house. The home was designed so that the North Star sits directly over the ridgepole of the front porch roof.

This gazebo, a popular wedding site, is located at the Temple Avenue Park, a 2.5-acre passive community recreational park located within the historic Temple Avenue residential district. The site is the former location of Newnan High School and Temple Avenue Elementary School. The park is bounded on the west side by the Male Academy Museum and features a large water fountain and a memorial to local veterans. The plaza includes a wall of honor with bronze plaques recognizing those who died as a direct result of enemy action, a granite monument, dedicated engraved bricks, and bronze statues.

Local judge Byron H. Mathews donated his collection of Civil War artifacts to the Newnan-Coweta Historical Society, and his contributions still make up the majority of the local collection. On display for years at the Male Academy Museum, the collection is being shifted to the Historic Newnan Depot for the sesquicentennial anniversary of the Battle of Brown's Mill in 2014.

The Merrill-Bone Home, located at 64 College Street, was built in 1893 by Harrison E. Merrill. The Victorian home is distinguished by its Eastlake features, a hand-carved front door with its "bird in the hand" motif, and bird-shaped brackets beneath the front porch roof. The home also has a turret, as well as stained glass adorning the exterior windows and dormer. A carriage house duplicating the style of the home was added in 1986.

This home on College Street is one of only two buildings remaining from the old College Temple School for Women. This building once served as the science laboratory, but has been a private residence since the school's closing. The roof of the unusual octagonal structure is topped with a cupola. The rear of the building was identical to the front and served as the entrance from the college green.

The Farmer Street Cemetery contains about 200 unmarked gravesites that may be part of one of the largest slave cemeteries in the United States. A 1923 map shows a "Negro Grave Yard" on the site. Later maps call it the "Colored Cemetery." William B. Berry was the original owner of the land, and he transferred ownership to Newnan Cotton Mills in 1888. The deed preserved right of access to the cemetery. The only marker left at the cemetery memorializes three-month-old Charlie Burch.

Brown's Mill Battlefield, located on Millard Farmer Road, has now been preserved as a county park. The battle was fought on July 30, 1864, by Union forces led by Edward M. McCook and Confederate cavalry led by Gen. Joseph Wheeler. The battlefield park opened in July 2013 and includes a mile of slate walking trail, another half-mile walking trail, and interpretive signs telling the story of the Battle of Brown's Mill.

ABOUT THE NEWNAN-COWETA HISTORICAL SOCIETY

The Newnan-Coweta Historical Society (NCHS) interprets and preserves the historical, cultural, and architectural heritage of Coweta County through its programs, exhibitions, and collections while serving, engaging, and educating the diverse communities of Coweta County and the surrounding region.

The historical society operates the Male Academy Museum, at the intersection of Temple Avenue and College Street; the McRitchie-Hollis Museum, at 74 Jackson Street; and the Historic Newnan Depot (Newnan History Center) on East Broad Street. Contact NCHS at P.O. Box 1001, Newnan, GA, 30264, or at (770) 251-0207, or visit its website at www.newnancowetahistoricalsociety.com.

The McRitchie-Hollis Museum, located at 74 Jackson Street, is the headquarters of the Newnan-Coweta Historical Society. The museum, open from 10:00 a.m. to 12:00 p.m. and 1:00 p.m. to 3:00 p.m. Tuesdays through Saturdays, features rotating exhibits that tell stories about the history of Coweta County. The home, originally built by Ellis and Mildred Arnall Peniston in 1937, is adjacent to the University of West Georgia satellite campus.

Visit us at
arcadiapublishing.com

www.ingramcontent.com/pod-product-compliance
Lightning Source LLC
Chambersburg PA
CBHW050706110426
42813CB00007B/2103